Cambridge Primary

Hodder Cambridge Primary
Science
Teacher's Pack

Stage 1

Rosemary Feasey

Series editor: Deborah Herridge

HODDER
EDUCATION
AN HACHETTE UK COMPANY

Acknowledgements

The Publisher is extremely grateful to the following schools for their comments and feedback during the development of this series:

Avalon Heights World Private School, Ajman
The Oxford School, Dubai
Al Amana Private School, Sharjah
British International School, Ajman
Wesgreen International School, Sharjah
As Seeb International School, Al Khoud

The publishers would like to thank the following for permission to reproduce copyright material:

p.44 http://www.grandparents.com/grandkids/activities-games-and-crafts/simon-says ("These instructions have been re-printed with the permission of the British Council and are taken from www.britishcouncil.or/learnenglishkids"); **p.45** https://learnenglishkids.britishcouncil.org/en/video-tips/simon-says ("These instructions have been re-printed with the permission of the British Council and are taken from www.britishcouncil.or/learnenglishkids"); **pp.51,102** http://www.insighttoptom. com.au/; **pp.94, 98** https://PicCollage.com/

Practice and quiz questions and answers have been written by the author(s).

Note: While every effort has been made to check the instructions for practical work described in this book carefully, schools should conduct their own risk assessments in accordance with local health and safety requirements.

Every effort has been made to trace all copyright holders, but if any have been inadvertently overlooked the Publishers will be pleased to make the necessary arrangements at the first opportunity.

Although every effort has been made to ensure that website addresses are correct at time of going to press, Hodder Education cannot be held responsible for the content of any website mentioned in this book. It is sometimes possible to find a relocated web page by typing in the address of the home page for a website in the URL window of your browser.

Hachette UK's policy is to use papers that are natural, renewable and recyclable products and made from wood grown in sustainable forests. The logging and manufacturing processes are expected to conform to the environmental regulations of the country of origin.

Orders: please contact Bookpoint Ltd, 130 Milton Park, Abingdon, Oxon OX14 4SB. Telephone: (44) 01235 827720. Fax: (44) 01235 400454. Lines are open from 9.00–5.00, Monday to Saturday, with a 24 hour message answering service. You can also order through our website www.hoddereducation.com

© Rosemary Feasey 2017

Published by Hodder Education

An Hachette UK Company

Carmelite House, 50 Victoria Embankment, London EC4Y 0DZ

Impression number   5 4 3 2 1

Year   2019 2018 2017

Cover illustration © Steve Evans

Illustrations by Jeanne du Plessis and Steve Evans

Typeset in FS Albert 11 on 13pt by Andrea Willmore

Printed in Great Britain by CPI Group (UK) Ltd, Croydon, CR0 4YY

A catalogue record for this title is available from the British Library

9781471883965

Contents

Introduction

About the series

Hodder Cambridge Primary Science is a series consisting of a Learner's Book, Teacher's Pack, Workbook and Digital Resource Pack for each stage of the Cambridge Primary Science curriculum framework.

The books are written by experienced primary practitioners to reflect the science mastery approach covering the Cambridge Primary Science curriculum framework. The content of each book is outlined below.

Learner's Book

The structure and content of the Learner's Book is based on the Cambridge Primary Science curriculum framework for each stage. There are three chapters in each Learner's Book: Biology, Chemistry and Physics, with a quiz at the end of each chapter. There are six units per Learner's Book. Units contain:

- key 'Scientific words'
- key information about the concept – 'Think like a scientist!'
- activities designed to build on learners' knowledge, skills and understanding
- question prompts to encourage independent thinking about the concept
- 'Talk partners' activities
- investigations to assess learners' ideas about the concept, with 'Be careful!' safety tips
- 'Challenge yourself!' activities to offer practice and extend learners' knowledge, skills and understanding of the concept
- links to the digital resource material when you see this icon
- self-assessment activities and checklist at the end of each unit.

Teacher's Pack

The Teacher's Pack supports the activities in the Learner's Book and Workbook, and reinforces the learning through:

- an objectives overview table for each unit
- a list of objectives for each section in the Learner's Book
- information about the topic under the heading 'Background information'
- activities and ideas to start the lesson under the heading 'Starter activity suggestions'
- notes and answers to match the Learner's Book, under the heading 'Activity notes and answers'
- answers to Workbook questions
- safety advice under the heading 'Be careful!'
- suggestions for success criteria
- ideas for further activities
- practice test answers for the three tests during the year
- ideas for assessment
- ICT ideas
- links to the digital resource materials where you see this icon
- photocopiable pages to support the concepts in the Learner's Book.

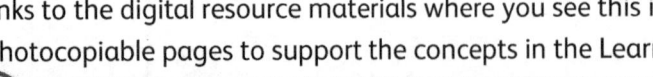  Workbook

- The Workbook can be used for homework or extension activities after completion of the relevant Learner's Book pages. The Workbook builds on what has taken place during the lesson. It also challenges learners to develop their understanding in more depth, demonstrating this understanding through:
  - activities linked to the objectives in the Learner's Book
  - a self-assessment checklist at the end of each unit.

Digital Resource Pack

The Digital Resource Pack supports the activities in the Learner's Book, Teacher's Pack and Workbook. These resources in the Digital Resource Pack reinforce learning through:

- slideshows
- video clips
- interactive activities
- photocopiable masters (PCM)
- an audio scientific dictionary.

How to use this series

Learners may complete the units in the Learner's Book in any order. Adopting the science mastery approach, each unit follows a progressive format to ensure full coverage of the objectives. Fully integrated scientific enquiry objectives in each unit provide learners with plenty of practice to master these framework requirements.

What is the mastery approach?

Mastery learning is rooted in the belief that all learners can succeed if given the right input, support and practice. The mastery approach is a teaching strategy, which aims to ensure that learners reach a prescribed level of understanding, being secure in their knowledge of a science concept or competent in a skill, before moving on to the next element of learning. The Cambridge Primary Science curriculum framework is a comprehensive mixture of science subject knowledge and practical scientific skills. The activities in the Learner's Book are designed to support all learners towards mastery.

Key elements of the mastery approach are:

Effective assessment for learning

Each unit begins with a series of activities that assess what learners already know and understand about the unit. These provide teachers with opportunities to assess learners' existing knowledge and skills in a particular curriculum area, and to check that learners are secure in existing ideas and skills before introducing new areas of learning. If learners hold any misconceptions or have incomplete understanding of an area of science, the teacher can address the knowledge gaps before introducing new learning.

Introducing new ideas and skills

New ideas are then introduced to learners in carefully sequenced steps. If learners have difficulties, the teacher offers different learning opportunities or focused teaching until learners master the skill or concept. Enough time is allocated to this process, rather than moving through learning quickly with only superficial understanding.

Practice and consolidation

Learners are given opportunities to practise the new ideas and skills so that they become confident and competent in them. This enables them to consolidate these ideas and skills by using them in different activities and contexts. Giving learners opportunities to practise their new skills or knowledge in different ways means that they develop scientific fluency. They are then able to move on to the next idea and skill with confidence.

Synthesising information

In each unit, learners are challenged to build on existing knowledge and understanding, and to combine this with recently introduced ideas to make secure progress.

Applying and re-applying knowledge, understanding and skills

Learners have frequent opportunities to apply knowledge, understanding and skills in a variety of contexts. Applying knowledge and skills in a new or different context enables teachers, and learners themselves, to assess how secure their knowledge, understanding and skills are. Application is important because it challenges learners to use what they know and to apply their skills in new situations. It also provides teachers with opportunities for assessing progress.

Reflection

Learners are asked to reflect on what they know and can do, individually and with their working partners or groups. Expectations of learning and criteria for successful learning and progress are made explicit to learners throughout. This helps learners to self-assess and to make judgements about what they need to learn next in order to progress. Reflection also offers learners the opportunity to celebrate their progress in scientific learning.

Common features in each unit

To support the mastery approach, each unit has been created to develop learners' mastery through the following common features:

- setting clear objectives so that all learners know what they are learning
- sharing explicit success criteria so learners can judge when they have achieved their learning objectives
- offering learning in small, carefully sequenced steps, breaking down learning into manageable, logical steps
- assessing what learners already know so that they revisit prior understanding, helping both teachers and learners to recognise what learners know and where they are less secure in their understanding
- providing examples of an idea in different ways to help to develop deeper understanding
- using precise and targeted questioning to check and further develop learners' understanding
- challenging learners to make connections between ideas so they gain deeper understanding
- using talk partners so that learners have to communicate their ideas and ways of working to someone else – hearing their own and others' ideas provides reinforcement or helps them to develop their own ideas further; it also provides opportunities for teachers to assess learning.

Scientific enquiry activities

There are different kinds of scientific enquiry activities, which help learners to develop different ideas and ways of working. In each unit, learners experience of a range of these types of activities, as explained in the examples in the table. The following examples are from Stage 1 and Stage 2.

Scientific enquiry activity	What does it mean?	Purpose	Examples
Observing (over time)	Learners will, for example, use all their senses (where relevant and safe) to observe change over different periods of time, from within a few minutes to an hour, day, week and over a year.	This is particularly important when observing change over longer periods of time to understand, for example, life cycles of animals and plants, the changes in day and night, and seasonal changes.	Learners will, for example: Observe how plants grow over time Measure plant growth over time. Learners will know that animals produce offspring which, over time, change and grow into adults.
Pattern seeking	Learners will, for example, observe patterns in data, numbers, looking for trends and related events in the natural world that cannot easily be controlled.	Patterns (particularly in numbers) can be used to identify a trend or relationships between one or more things.	Learners will, for example: Collect measurements about the weather and notice patterns in data, such as when the hottest and coolest months are. Learners will, for example, observe themselves: *Are the oldest learners the tallest? Do the learners with the longest feet have the longest arms?*
Identifying, classifying and grouping	**Grouping** – sorting according to similar observable features or behaviours, such as size, shape, number of legs. **Classifying** – sorting according to a scientific grouping, such as vertebrate groups, type of material. It helps to order a group of things based usually on similarities rather than differences. **Identifying** – giving a scientific name to something, such as petal, seed, plastic, pumice.	Classification is the method used by scientists to order living organisms and materials.	Learners will, for example: Group things that are alive and have never been alive. Group common materials by their properties, such as soft, hard, dull, shiny. Identify and name parts of a plant and parts of the human body.

Scientific enquiry activity	What does it mean?	Purpose	Examples
Comparative testing	This method is where two or more objects are compared, but not in a way that links cause and effect. This is useful when the variables (factors) are categoric rather than continuous.	Comparative tests for younger children may involve a similar method and process to fair testing but they will be comparing categoric variables (factors) rather than demonstrating causal relationships. Many of these examples may take the form of finding the best material for a particular purpose.	Learners will, for example: Compare which of their eyes they see with the best. Compare and describe sounds from different sources. Investigate the hardness of rocks – which rock scratches another.
Fair testing (controlled investigations)	A fair test answers a scientific question in a systematic way. It seeks to link cause and effect. It examines the effect that changing one variable (factor) has on another while keeping all other conditions the same. Fair tests are only appropriate to use when exploring variables (factors) that are continuous and can be changed, such as the surface area of a parachute. Fair tests are not suitable for investigating natural phenomena like the weather or living things such as ourselves as we cannot change variables (factors) in a systematic way.	Learners collect data to identify and explain the relationship between two variables (factors). This is not always fully applicable to these stages although you can begin to introduce the principles of the method in other forms of enquiry. Learners would not be expected to devise their own test at Stages 1 and 2.	Learners ask questions, such as: Does the sound of the teacher's whistle change the further we go away from it? When we change the slope of a ramp, what happens to how far the toy car travels?
Researching using secondary sources	This means finding out information using books, watching videos, using the internet, reading leaflets, asking an expert, etc.	This is an appropriate approach to answering questions which are impossible or unsafe for learners to answer using first-hand experiences. This type of enquiry enables learners to compare and evaluate information from multiple sources and distinguish opinion from fact. It also leads to an understanding that sometimes in science questions do not have definitive answers.	Learners might use a book or the internet to find out about: animals in different countries different planets in the solar system.

Helping learners to retain information

Language

Learners are introduced to scientific language throughout each unit. New terms are highlighted in bold and placed in a 'Scientific words' box. Once introduced, the words may be used frequently in the unit, so that learners have opportunities for repetition to reinforce the word and its meaning. When learners write or talk about specific ideas and ways of working, they are prompted to use specific vocabulary to ensure that they use key words regularly. This reinforces links between language and ideas and ways of working.

- **Spelling** – learners are expected to learn how to spell key scientific words and use them regularly. There are also activities that engage learners in, for example, word searches, crosswords and identifying jumbled words; this supports learners in learning key scientific words.

- **Revisit, reinforce** – a range of strategies are used so that learners regularly revisit ideas and ways of working; understanding is reinforced and becomes embedded.

- **Different contexts** – across a unit, learners meet concepts and ways of working scientifically in different contexts. For example, in Stage 1, there are activities where learners find out about materials and use their knowledge to solve the problem of mopping up spills at a party. This helps learners to appreciate that ideas are used in many ways and places in their lives. This is also important for checking their learning, if they can apply learning to a new context appropriately this provides useful assessment evidence.

How mastery comes across in the classroom

The units are designed so that learners are engaged in practical activities wherever appropriate. These hands-on experiences demand that they use and apply their understanding and skills. In science, learners are expected to develop increasing independence. Teachers should encourage them to become more able to work on their own, with a partner or in a small group.

Pattern of each unit

Each unit follows a general pattern for teaching and consolidating the unit objectives, for example:

- Units begin with a learner-led practical activity to re-introduce the concept/objectives from previous learning linked to the topic. The purpose of these activities is to find out what learners already know, for example, with the use of talk partners. Here teachers can assess how much learners already know or have retained about a scientific topic, and if they have the confidence to move on to new learning. If they are not quite ready, offer some quick activities to revise and consolidate, before moving on to the next step in the unit.

- Learners are introduced to new ideas and ways of working scientifically. The teacher's role here is to encourage learners to engage in activities and share their learning with you, talk partners and the rest of the class. Asking relevant questions, listening to learners, observing what they do, and reading what they write, mean that the teacher is continually assessing progress and deciding whether to go over a key idea again or to progress to the next idea.

- At all times, the teacher will expect all learners to use the key words from the scientific words boxes in the Learner's Book. This way, they will become confident in using scientific vocabulary.

- Many activities ask learners to share their ideas or findings with other groups. This approach challenges learners to make sense of their ideas and communicate effectively, as well as listen to and reflect on what other groups say.

Conducting fair test investigations in the classroom

Fair test questions are put to learners in relevant units. At other times, learners are asked to think about a question that they would like to investigate. It is important that learners are given thinking and planning time before starting to carry out their fair test. This allows them to make decisions about:

- *What does the question mean?*
- *What should be changed?*
- *What should be kept the same?*
- *What needs to be measured?*
- *How should the results be recorded?*

You can find a detailed explanation of this approach on pages 4 and 5 of the Learner's Book.

Predicting

In science, we often ask learners to think about what will happen; this is called a prediction. In very young learners these are often just guesses because they have limited or no experience to draw upon. The more experiences they have, the more able they are to offer predictions that have their origins in prior knowledge. For example, if learners have explored different materials and tested to see if they are waterproof, they will be more able to predict accurately which materials will keep their toy rabbit dry.

Planning their own fair test investigations

Most units do not demand that learners write lengthy plans about how they will carry out a fair test. Experience shows that this can disadvantage learners who are less confident in writing. Some plans are also changed, as learners make sense of the equipment and realise that their ideas will not work. Let learners:

- talk to each other, to share ideas and decide which ideas might best answer their question
- have a trial run of different aspects (if possible), to make sure that they will work.

Carrying out their own fair test investigations

Here, learners will need teacher support in the form of careful questioning. This will help learners to think about what they are doing, rather than the teacher saying, 'It will not work' or 'Do it this way'. These question examples should help to support and develop learners to work independently:

- *What do you think will happen if you do that?*
- *How have you made your test fair?*
- *What kind of measurements will you need?*
- *What do you think will be the best way to record your results?*

Drawing conclusions

Ensure that after finishing the practical part of their investigation, learners have time to look at their results and draw a conclusion. They must think about their results, to be able to answer their original question or solve a problem. Suggest that it might be easier for them to move their results (data) from a table to a graph. This table shows an easy way to tell if a graph should be a bar chart or a line graph.

What I changed	What I measured	Type of graph
Thing	Number	Bar chart
Number	Number	Line graph

Teachers can support this by asking questions such as:

- *Tell the story of your graph. What happens to the bars or the lines?*
- *What is the pattern of your graph?*
- *Are there any strange results that do not seem to fit? Where? What do you think might be the reason? Use your data to answer your question and draw your conclusion.*
- *Was your prediction right or wrong? How do you know?*

New questions from fair test investigations

Once the investigation is complete and learners have been supported to think about and make sense of their results, ask them if there is anything else that they would like to find out and test. For example, if they are exploring stretchy materials they might ask:

- *Which fabric is the stretchiest?*
- *Are thin fabrics stretchier than thick fabrics?*

By giving learners opportunities to ask and answer new questions of their own, they extend their own learning and apply ideas to new situations. This indicates a mastery of an idea and skill.

Scientific equipment needed for Stage 1

This list shows items that you will need in addition to basic classroom resources such as pencils, pens, crayons, rulers, A4 and A3 sheets of paper, card (thin and thick, in different sizes), scissors, glue, etc.

Unit 1: old magazines; pictures of real and artificial plants; plants; hand lenses; area with plants for plant hunt; fruits and vegetables; spoons; knives; seeds; soil; plant pots; clear plastic pots; card cones; clean junk materials; photographs or drawings of learners' faces.

Unit 2: string; mirrors; blindfolds; flowers; hand lenses; small pieces of materials with different textures; objects with different textures; bags or boxes for hiding objects; six small pots with different things to smell (such as herbs, garlic, spices, flowers, coffee, juice and vinegar); fruits with different smells; substances for learners to make pots with horrible smells; pieces of foods with different sweet, sour and salty tastes; mint sweets; things for making sounds; sound boxes.

Unit 3: materials for making models of duck habitats (such as trays, soil, water, plastic, toy ducks, grass, pebbles); materials for making frog life cycles (such as paper plates and dough); photographs of people at different ages; paper plates; uncooked pasta shapes; different fruits; wooden skewers; mirrors.

Unit 4: objects made from different materials (metal, wood, plastic, glass, fabric); boxes; wooden lolly sticks; small containers; fabric scraps; materials for mopping up spills (such as paper towels, dishcloths, sponges).

Unit 5: scrap materials or building materials for making pull-along toys; materials for making box cars (such as large boxes); plastic water bottles for making skittles; pebbles or sand; balls; squeezy bottles for squirting; table tennis balls; straws; bubble wands; bubble mixture; paper bags; hole punches; paper strips or ribbons; wool or string.

Unit 6: a few musical instruments; different materials for sound boards (such as cardboard, sandpaper, bubble wrap, sweet wrappers, straws); small containers; different small objects; earmuffs; funnels; plastic bottles; beads or buttons; paints; drums; scrap materials; objects that are sound makers; sand timers.

Safety advice

Where appropriate, safety warnings are identified and explained in the Teacher's Pack, and in the Learner's Book (under the heading 'Be careful!'). Teachers are responsible for ensuring that activities are checked to ensure that they are safe. The notes act as a warning to consider specific safety issues, but the teacher must check equipment and materials used in the classroom to make sure that safe practices are followed at all times. This series is purchased by many different countries, so teachers must make sure that, for example, plants and foods used in science lessons are safe. It is also important to check which learners may have food allergies, before purchasing or using foodstuffs.

It is good practice to encourage learners to think about working carefully and safely. They should make sure that they, and others with whom they are working, are safe. Before starting an activity, ask learners to discuss with their partners or others in the group, what might be a hazard and could be harmful. Then ask how they will work to make sure that they stay safe.

When using the internet for research, ensure that learners understand how to be safe online before starting the activity.

Assessment

Learning objectives

An overview of all the objectives with their codes is provided at the beginning of each unit in the Teacher's Pack. It is good practice to share these objectives with learners at the beginning of each lesson in learner-friendly language. This will ensure that they are clear on the focus of each activity and what they are expected to learn. At the end of each lesson, ask learners to reflect on what they have learned and to check their understanding against the success criteria.

Background information

This section explains the purpose of the learning and gives key knowledge and understanding that is covered in the following activities. This also supports teacher assessment of learners.

Assessing learners' prior understanding and misconceptions

At the beginning of each unit, the purpose of the starter activities in the Teacher's Pack and the first page of activities in the Learner's Book is to revisit previous learning linked to the unit. The activities will help the teacher to assess how confident learners are and check for misconceptions. These can then be identified and remedied before continuing with new learning in the unit. The activities are also used to remind learners of previous learning that they will be using in the new unit.

Success criteria

In each section of the teacher's notes, suggestions for success criteria are given. The success criteria are used to assess the outcome of the learning that has taken place. The success criteria are, in effect, what the successful learning will 'look' like once the learning objectives have been met. For example, for Stage 1 Unit 1 (Learner's Book pages 6–7), the success criteria are:

While completing the activities, assess and record learners who can:
- say that plants are living things
- name some things that are living and some that have never been alive
- make comparisons between things that are alive and things that have never been alive.

You could ask learners to write the success criteria at the top of their work. Then ask them to reflect on how well, for example, they can sort living things into groups and explain their groupings.

Formative assessment

Formative assessment is a form of ongoing assessment that occurs in every lesson. It informs the teacher and the learner of the progress that they are making, linked to the success criteria.

Formative assessment is important because it means that teachers and learners are continually reflecting on how the learning is moving forward. Where necessary, teachers can work with learners during the lesson, to support any issues in learning that emerge.

Formative assessment should be used to inform the next steps in learning, and may influence changes in planning and therefore the next lessons. Formative assessment is a cycle: finding out what learners know, moving learning forward, finding out how that learning has changed (what they know now) and planning the next steps. Where you find that learners are still unsure, stop and take time to revisit an idea or skill, and change the activity or context. Move on to new learning when learning is secure. Assessment is about you (and learners) continually reflecting on learning, and ensuring that teaching is in line with learning.

Teachers and learners can assess learning easily, in many ways. These are built into units, for example:

- **Talk partners** – are used regularly throughout each unit to encourage learners, in pairs or groups, to talk about their learning. In this way, they can articulate their ideas and listen to each other. Where appropriate, they can adjust what they are thinking and saying. The teacher's role is to move around the classroom, listening to learners talking to one another, to identify how learning is taking place. Teachers can provide support where ideas may need modelling (demonstrating with an example), or offer new challenges to those learners who are secure in their thinking and ways of working.

- **Fact cards and definitions** – across the units, learners are often asked to carry out short activities such as creating fact cards, completing sentences, or creating their own definitions for key scientific words. These activities help learners to consolidate their learning. They enable teachers to assess learning, and especially, the use of scientific language. Sometimes learners are asked to solve 'What am I?' puzzles. These are a fun way of providing formative assessment opportunities.

- **Application activities** – are usually towards the end of a unit, when learners engage in activities that require them to apply their learning in different contexts or solve a problem. These are important because teachers can assess better whether learning is secure by checking if learners can apply it to a different or new situation.

Summative assessment

Summative assessment is placed at the end of each unit in the Learner's Book to assess at a key point in time, what learners know, understand and can do. There are Practice tests and self-assessment checklists in the Learner's Books, and self-assessment pages in the Workbooks, which form part of the summative assessment process.

The information gained from both the formative and summative assessments should be used to inform future planning in order to close any gaps in learners' understanding and skills. Remember that assessment is ongoing. It is built into all units and should not be viewed as something separate, or only to be done when a unit is finished.

Strategies for differentiation

While the mastery approach intends for all learners to reach the same levels of understanding and security of knowledge before moving on, teachers may need to use a different approach for some learners or spend additional practice time with learners who have specific learning challenges.

Differentiation means changing the teaching and learning process so that the different needs of learners can be accommodated and individual learning maximised. It involves giving learners tasks that best fit their abilities while meeting the same learning criteria as their peers. For example, groups of learners could be given slightly different tasks to complete, they might be given more time to complete a task, or they could work with an adult who can support them. This will allow all learners to achieve the same learning objectives, but they will reach the goal in slightly different ways.

Keeping it practical

Wherever possible, across all units, learning has been made as practical as possible, so that learners have hands-on experience of ideas and developing skills. Many learners need concrete hands-on experiences to help them learn and this is a key feature of activities across units.

Breaking down ideas

Concepts, for example, the parts of a plant, are broken down into small steps so that learners are guided through a concept in a way that is manageable for most learners. By using these small steps, and by mastering each small step, we can build to secure understanding of the bigger concept.

Some ideas for specific age groups cannot easily be broken down into small steps because of the type of concept. For example, a magnet either attracts a material or it does not. However, you can give learners opportunities to explore magnets in different ways to help them understand this concept.

Repetition, reinforcement

This is important for all learners, but it does help some learners who need to meet an idea more than once or in a different form to consolidate learning.

Talk partners

Using talk partners provides opportunities for learners to think about and articulate their ideas according to their own level of understanding. By talking about their thinking, learners often change their ideas as they listen to someone else or because they hear their own thoughts.

Challenge yourself!

'Challenge yourself!' questions are in all units. Their intention is to extend and challenge learners who are confident with an idea, by presenting a challenge question that they can explore or research.

Application activities

Application activities are usually found towards the end of a unit. They are an important part of the mastery approach, as they provide opportunities to apply new learning and contexts that have not been used in the unit. They are often problem-solving type activities, or design and make. Teachers can fine-tune these for different learners where necessary.

Rosemary Feasey and Deborah Herridge (Series editors)

Unit 1 Plants

Objectives overview

Learning objective	Objective code	Learner's Book pages	Teacher's Pack pages	Workbook pages	Digital Resource Pack
Biology: Plants					
Know that plants are living things	1Bp1	6, 7, 8, 9, 10, 11, 14, 16, 26, 27	17, 18, 19, 20, 21, 22, 23, 26, 27, 38, 39	4, 5, 6	Unit 1 slides 3, 4, 6, PCM1
Know that there are living things and things that have never been alive	1Bp2	6, 7, 8, 9	17, 18, 19, 20, 21	4, 5, 6	Unit 1 slide 3, PCM1
Explore ways that different animals and plants inhabit local environments	1Bp3	23, 24	34, 35, 36, 37	13	
Name the major parts of a plant, looking at real plants and models	1Bp4	12, 13, 14, 16, 26, 27	24, 25, 26, 27, 38, 39	7, 8, 14, 15	Unit 1 PCM2, interactive activity
Know that plants need light and water to grow	1Bp5	17, 18, 19, 20, 21, 26, 27	28, 29, 30, 31, 32, 33, 38, 39	9, 10, 11	Unit 1 slide 6
Explore how seeds grow into flowering plants	1Bp6	15, 17, 18, 19, 22, 23	28, 29, 30, 31, 34, 35	9, 10, 12	Unit 1 slides 5, 6, 7, video clip
Scientific enquiry: Ideas and evidence					
Try to answer questions by collecting evidence through observation	1Ep1	10, 11, 12, 13, 14, 15, 16, 17, 18, 19, 20, 21, 22, 23	22, 23, 24, 25, 26, 27, 28, 29, 30, 31, 32, 33, 34, 35	5, 7, 8, 9	Unit 1 slides 4, 5, 6
Scientific enquiry: Plan investigative work					
Ask questions and contribute to discussions about how to seek answers	1Ep2	20, 21	32, 33	10, 11	Unit 1 slides 5, 6
Make predictions	1Ep3	17, 18, 19, 21	28, 29, 30, 31	10, 11	
Decide what to do to try to answer a science question	1Ep4	20, 21	32, 33	10, 11	

Learning objective	Objective code	Learner's Book pages	Teacher's Pack pages	Workbook pages	Digital Resource Pack
Scientific enquiry: Obtain and present evidence					
Explore and observe in order to collect evidence (measurements and observations) to answer questions	1Eo1	10, 11, 12, 13, 14, 15, 16, 22, 23, 24	22, 23, 24, 25, 26, 27, 34, 35, 36, 37	6, 7, 8, 12, 13, 14	Unit 1 slide 7
Suggest ideas and follow instructions	1Eo2	14, 15, 17, 18	26, 27, 28, 29, 30, 31	9	
Record stages in work	1Eo3	16, 17, 20, 21, 22, 24, 25	28, 29, 32, 33, 34, 35, 36, 37	11	
Scientific enquiry: Consider evidence and approach					
Make comparisons	1Eo4	6, 7, 8, 9, 10, 11, 12, 13, 16, 20, 21, 22, 23, 24, 25	17, 18, 19, 20, 21, 22, 23, 24, 25, 28, 29, 32, 33, 34, 35, 36, 37	4, 5, 6, 12, 13, 14	Unit 1 slides 3, 4
Compare what happened with predictions	1Eo5	20, 21	32, 33		
Model and communicate ideas in order to share, explain and develop them	1Eo6	18, 19, 24, 25	30, 31, 36, 37	10, 11, 13, 14	

Living things

 Learner's Book
pages 6–7

 Workbook
page 4

 Digital Resource

Objectives

- Know that plants are living things. (1Bp1)
- Know that there are living things and things that have never been alive. (1Bp2)
- Make comparisons. (1Eo4)

Background information

The aim of the activities on pages 6 and 7 of the Learner's Book is to find out what learners know about living things, specifically what they know about the concepts of things that are alive or have never been alive. In science, everything in the world can be classified into 'living' (alive), 'not alive' and 'has never been alive'. In Stage 1, the focus is on 'alive' and 'has never been alive'. A living thing (alive) carries out life processes: it moves (on its own), it reacts to its surroundings, it needs air, it feeds, it grows, it reproduces and it gets rid of waste. In later stages, learners will remember life processes using the mnemonic MRS GREN (movement, reproduction, sensitivity, growth, respiration, excretion and nutrition). In Stage 1, learners are introduced to the idea that things that are alive carry out the following processes: eat, move, breathe, grow and use their senses. (In later stages, reproduction and excretion are added.)

Those things that have never been alive have never carried out the life processes, so rocks, metal and plastic have never been alive. The term 'not alive' relates to those things in the world that were once alive but no longer are. For example, fallen leaves on the ground were once alive as part of living trees, paper is made from wood, and wood was once alive as a tree. Objects such as stones, rocks and a lamp post were never alive, because they were never able to carry out the life processes.

Starter activity suggestions

- Give learners toy animals and ask them to talk about whether or not they think these animals are alive. They should give reasons for their answers. At this stage, it does not matter if they are correct or not. What is more important is that you elicit their ideas.
- Ask learners to talk with their partners about how they know that each one of them is alive. Collect ideas from the class.
- Display the Unit 1 digital resource slideshow 1, slide 3: Alive or not alive? Use it to gather ideas of what learners know about things that are alive or not alive. Ask learners to explain why they think the things shown are either alive or not.

 Unit 1 slideshow, slide 3: Alive or not alive?

Answers to slide 3:
a tree, plant, giraffe, baby
b car, can of soda, chair, spoon
c They are things that carry out life processes, i.e. eat, move, breathe, grow and use their senses.

- To make the experience more practical, place a range of items on tables for learners to sort, such as stones, pictures of animals, a live potted plant and plastic objects. Plastic animals have not been included here. This will avoid learners becoming confused between the material plastic never having been alive and the idea that the animals represent living things.

Activity notes and answers

Page 6 Activity 1
Answers:
a A – trees (forest)   B – bird (parakeet)   C – elephant   D – butterfly on flower
b Accept appropriate descriptions of the living things in the picture. The idea is for the learners to familiarise themselves with each living thing.

Page 6 Talk partners Support learners in talking about the word *alive* through use of questions such as: *What do things that are alive do? Are you alive? How do you know? What other things at home or around our school are alive?*

Page 6 Activity 2
Answers:
a Accept any responses from the learners. The aim is to elicit their ideas to find out what they are thinking. Ask learners to explain their answers by asking some questions, such as: *Why do you think the cat is alive?*
b Accept any responses from the learners. The aim is to elicit their ideas to find out what they are thinking. Ask learners to explain their answers by asking some questions, such as: *Why do you think the car is not alive?* This will help you to understand their reasoning, rather than just taking the answers at face value.
c Accept any responses from learners about what living things can do. The aim is to elicit their ideas to find out what they are thinking.

Page 6 Talk partners
Answers:
a Accept any responses from the learners. The aim is to elicit their ideas to find out what they are thinking. Do ask learners if they agree with each other, and what their reasons are for any differences in answers.
b Accept any responses from the learners. The aim is to elicit their ideas to find out what they are thinking. Ask learners if they agree with each other and probe understanding by asking: *I wonder what would happen if…* or *Does that mean the computer can move?*

How do we know something is alive?

 Activity notes and answers

Page 7 Activity 1
Answers:
a elephant A   b elephant B   c no
d Accept any responses from the learners. Listen to how they know whether a toy elephant has ever been alive or not alive, in order to support learners moving forward. If they understand the concept, their answers will include, for example, that it has never been alive because the toy elephant has never been able to breathe, move, eat or grow.

Further activities

- Ask learners to complete Workbook page 4: Alive or not alive?

- Give learners magazines and catalogues to cut up and stick pictures into sets, either *Alive* and *Not alive*. Make sure that the pictures include plants, as well as animals and objects.

- Use the Unit 1 digital resource PCM1: Alive or not alive? Copy it onto card and cut the pictures out to create a sorting game. Give learners the headings *Alive* and *Not alive* and ask them to sort the pictures.

 Unit 1 PCM1: Alive or not alive?

Answers to PCM1:
Alive: fish, spider, tree, plant, frog, baby.
Not alive: chair, computer, glass, car, cup, puddle.

- Play a 'What next' game. Start the game yourself by saying *Alive*, followed by saying the name of someone in the class. That person gives the name of something alive, then says either *Alive* or *Not alive*, followed by the name of someone else in the class. If the person says *Not alive*, the next person must name something that is not alive. Learners continue taking turns in the same way, until you think that their concentration is waning.

 ICT links

- Give learners a camera to take six photographs of things around the classroom and/or school grounds that are alive or not alive.
- Challenge learners to take a video of three things that are alive and three things that are not alive. They must also say which is which.

Assessment ideas

Use the Unit 1 digital resource slideshow, slide 3: Alive or not alive? as an initial assessment to find out what learners already know about things that are alive or not alive. Then use the information to decide on the next step in your teaching process.

 Unit 1 slideshow, slide 3: Alive or not alive?

Success criteria

While completing the activities, assess and record learners who can:

- say that plants are living things
- name some things that are living and some that have never been alive
- make comparisons between things that are living and things that have never been alive.

 Workbook answers

Page 4 Alive or not alive?
1 Alive: lizard, human, tree, plant, giraffe
2 Check learners' drawings.

Alive or never alive?

 Learner's Book
pages 8–9

 Workbook
page 5

Objectives

- Know that plants are living things. (1Bp1)
- Know that there are living things and things that have never been alive. (1Bp2)
- Make comparisons. (1Eo4)

Background information

The purpose of the activities on pages 8 and 9 of the Learner's Book is to introduce learners to the concept that something is a living thing if it can eat, move (on its own), breathe, grow and use its senses. These pages will also support those learners who already have some knowledge through repetition of this idea.

Learners will benefit from being offered examples of 'alive' and 'never alive' in as many contexts as possible. Ensure that examples include both animals and plants, so that learners do not develop the misconception that plants are not living things.

By eliciting learners' ideas throughout this unit, these formative assessment opportunities help to indicate whether learners require additional experiences to ensure that they are secure in their ideas before moving on.

Starter activity suggestions

- Provide groups with collections of objects and pictures to sort into *Alive* and *Not alive* groups. Make sure that they justify, with reasons, their thinking to each other. If the group cannot agree, encourage them to place the objects or pictures in a separate 'not sure' group.
- Give learners a large sheet of paper on which to write the names of things that are alive and not alive. Alternatively, they can draw these things. Give each member of the group a pen, so that they can all contribute. Encourage them to discuss one another's contributions.

Activity notes and answers

Page 8 Activity 1
Answers:
a Alive – B plant growing, E older person, F tree. Never been alive – A mobile phone, C cup, D robot.
b Help learners to think about themselves and the idea that living things eat, move, breathe, grow and can have young (babies).

Page 8 Activity 2 Check how learners have sorted their pictures. Ask them to justify their reasons, so that you can find out the reasoning behind how they have sorted.

Plants are alive

Activity notes and answers

Page 9 Activity 1
Answers:
a Sunflower A is alive; sunflower B has never been alive.
b Learners might suggest that real flowers (flowers that are alive) do not have faces. The second flower has a cartoon face, which shows that it is not alive.

Further activities

- Ask learners to complete Workbook page 5: Find out!

- Provide learners with a collection of plants that are alive in pots, as well as artificial plants, such as fabric or plastic plants. This will allow learners to compare the plants directly. Include in comparisons how the plants feel (for example, touch different plants). Guide learners in looking for features such as roots.

- Take learners into the school grounds for an 'It's alive/Not alive' hunt. Working in pairs, learners hunt for objects that are not alive to put into a small container, such as a plastic film canister, matchbox or small tin. Tell learners the rules are that each item must fit into the container and that they cannot repeat any objects. When they have completed their collections, they must then search the grounds for anything that is alive. (This could include evidence that something alive has been there, such as feathers.) Tell them that we must never harm living things. They will therefore draw or photograph the things that are alive to share with other groups, rather than collecting them. The different groups then talk to each other about their collections, as well as about how they know that some things are not alive and others are.

- Use their collections back in the classroom. Ask learners to glue them onto card or paper. They should annotate or write a sentence to say how they know that these things are not alive.

Success criteria

While completing the activities, assess and record learners who can:

- say that plants are living things
- name some things that are living and some that have never been alive
- make comparisons between a flower that is alive and one that has never been alive.

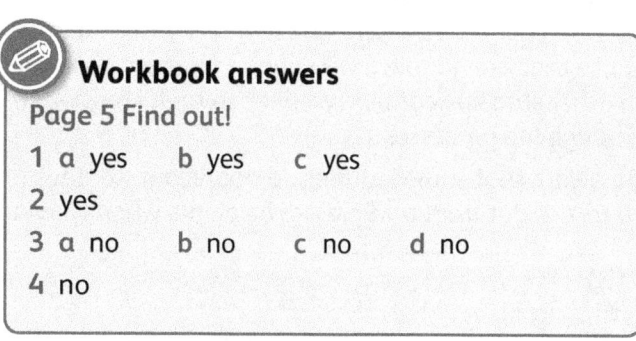

Workbook answers

Page 5 Find out!

1 a yes   b yes   c yes
2 yes
3 a no   b no   c no   d no
4 no

Who do you agree with?

Learner's Book
pages 10–11

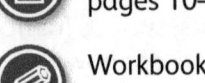

Workbook
page 6

Digital Resource

Objectives

- Know that plants are living things. (1Bp1)
- Try to answer questions by collecting evidence through observation. (1Ep1)
- Explore and observe in order to collect evidence (measurements and observations) to answer questions. (1Eo1)
- Make comparisons. (1Eo4)

Background information

The purpose of the activities on pages 10 and 11 of the Learner's Book is to consolidate the concept that plants are alive; they are living things. Learners may require experience of observing and talking about plants. Unlike themselves and other animals, they cannot see and therefore cannot experience plants carrying out life processes, such as feeding, moving, breathing (respiration), growing and being sensitive to their environment. Offering learners easily identifiable comparisons between plants that are living and those that are not alive will support learners in developing their ideas about plants. Later in this unit (and in other stages), learners will deepen their knowledge of plants and the idea that they are living things through life processes.

Be aware that some learners do not recognise trees and grass as being plants. You will therefore need to talk about trees and grasses as plants when viewing photographs and observing plants outdoors.

Starter activity suggestions

- Take the class outside to look at plants that are alive. Focus learners' attention on what they look and feel like, whether they can see roots, and so on. Guide them towards identifying changes in plants, such as a plant that they have observed growing and changing during the year.
- While outside, ask learners to think about what they need to stay alive. Ask them to think about what the plants need and how the plants get, for example, water. Listen to their ideas.
- Dig up a plant to show learners the roots. Talk about the roots taking up water. Make sure that you carefully put the plant back into the soil to continue growing.
- Ask learners how we can know that a plant moves. For example, talk about how some flowers turn their heads to face the Sun or open up in the morning and close at night. Talk about sensitive plants, such as sundews and the Venus flytrap, which move when they are touched.
- Back in class, show time-lapse sequences of flower buds opening from the internet, if possible.

ICT links

If possible, ask learners to take photographs of, or make a video, of five different plants. You can then use these alongside the Learner's Book activities on page 11 to support learning about different kinds of plants. Make sure that you talk about trees and grass as being plants.

Activity notes and answers

Page 10 Talk partners Ask groups to discuss what the two boys say and decide which one they agree with and why. Ask learners to share their ideas with other groups. At this stage, the aim is to encourage learners to share and discuss ideas. For some learners, this approach might lead to them changing their initial thinking. Write their ideas onto a chalkboard or whiteboard and talk through each one, asking learners to think about whether the idea works for plants.

Page 10 Activity 1
Answers:
Check that learners have sorted the plants they have been given into the correct sets. Ask them to explain why they have put the plants in each group.

Different plants

 Activity notes and answers

Page 11 Activity 1 Check that learners choose different plants which include trees and grasses. Ask them to say why plants are alive to assess their knowledge at this point.

Page 11 Challenge yourself! If learners bring photographs, drawings or written material to class, give them time to share it with others. Alternatively, place their work from home in a 'class book' or a display.

Further activities

- Ask learners to complete Workbook page 6: Spot the living things.
- Display the Unit 1 digital resource slideshow, slide 4: Biggest and smallest. Discuss the photographs of the largest and smallest flowering plants. Ask learners to share their thinking about each of the pictures. The sequoia can grow up to 85 m high. While Stage 1 learners are yet to learn about standard measures, you could take them into the school grounds and mark out 85 metres by letting everyone walk 85 big steps, counting together so that they get some idea of the size in relation to themselves.

 Unit 1 slideshow, slide 4: Biggest and smallest

Answers to slide 4:
a They show the largest tree and flower in the world: the sequoia tree and the rafflesia flower. They also show the small blue forget-me-not flower. Learners can see how small it is by comparing it to the ladybird.
b This will depend on your own school grounds.

- Take the class into the school grounds to count how many different plants they can find. Make sure that they include grasses and trees. Ask them to photograph the different plants, if possible, or draw them. Explain to them how to keep a simple tally chart to record the number of different plants they find.
- Challenge learners to find plants that are taller and smaller than they are, using comparative language from mathematics. Learners could stand next to plants and ask their partner to take a photograph showing the comparison between themselves and the plant. Alternatively, they could take a 'selfie' photograph.
- Challenge learners to solve the problem of how to prove which is the tallest plant in the school grounds.

Success criteria

While completing the activities, assess and record learners who can:
- say why plants are living things
- answer questions by using their observations of plants
- say that trees and grasses are plants
- say that plants can be big or small
- measure plants to see if they are bigger or smaller than themselves
- compare different plants to say if they are taller or shorter.

 Workbook answers

Page 6 Spot the living things

1 cat, boy, girl, birds, trees, flowers, grass

The parts of a plant

Learner's Book
pages 12–13

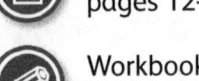

Workbook
page 7

Digital Resource

Objectives

- Name the major parts of a plant, looking at real plants and models. (1Bp4)
- Try to answer questions by collecting evidence through observation. (1Ep1)
- Explore and observe in order to collect evidence (measurements and observations) to answer questions. (1Eo1)
- Make comparisons. (1Eo4)

Background information

The purpose of the activities on pages 12 and 13 of the Learner's Book is to introduce learners to the names of basic parts of a plant, including leaf, flower, stem and roots.

- Roots grow downwards into the soil and take up water. The roots also anchor the plant, keeping it in the ground. By using a hand lens or a digital microscope, learners will be able to see the root/s and the root hairs.
- The stem is the stalk of the plant which helps the plant to stay upright. The stem carries water from the roots to the leaves. It also carries food made in the leaves to the other parts of the plant.
- The flowers make seeds which become new plants. Buds are the early stages of flowers. The leaves make food for the plant.

You could extend learners' knowledge of parts of a plant by including parts of a tree. Explain that trees have a stem, but we usually call it the trunk of a tree. Tree leaves are usually found on twigs and branches.

Prior to the activities on these pages, teach learners how to use a hand lens or digital microscope. The hand lens should be kept close to the eye and the object brought towards it until the learners can see it clearly.

One of the aims of Stage 1 is for learners to be able to read and spell basic scientific vocabulary. This provides the foundation for speaking and writing in science across all future stages. Every opportunity should be taken to help learners practise saying and spelling science words, particularly those identified in the scientific word boxes in the Learner's Book.

Starter activity suggestions

- Give learners plants in pots and teach them how to gently take the plant out of the pot to observe the different parts, especially the roots, using a hand lens. Make sure that learners understand that plants are living things. Plants therefore need to be handled with care, and must be carefully returned to the pot so that they can continue to grow.
- Ask learners to paint, draw and/or take photographs of the plant after it has been taken out of the pot. They must also label the different parts of the plant.

Activity notes and answers

Page 12 Activity 1 This could be a whole class activity where everyone says the words together. Some of the words, such as *stem*, can be said phonetically to help learners read the word.

Page 12 Activity 2 Listen to the learners commenting on what they can see using the hand lens. Remind them to use the correct scientific words for the parts of the plant. Encourage further observation by asking: *What else can you see? What is the most interesting thing you can see? What surprised you?*

The learners should be able to see the root hairs on the roots. Introduce this term to them. (Some learners may notice that some plants have one main root and others a network of smaller roots. This will be explained further in later stages.)

Page 12 Talk partners Ask learners to tell you when their partner can spell all of the words correctly. Learners could also find the names of other parts of a plant, such as petals, to learn to spell.

Page 12 Challenge yourself! Learners could write the words to take home on a slip of paper. Parents or carers should tick, comment or add a smiley face if they have heard the words being spelled correctly.

Going on a plant hunt

 Activity notes and answers

Page 13 Activity 1 During the plant hunt, learners should correctly use the hand lens to look at different plants. They should then share their observations with other learners. Remind everyone to use the scientific names of the different parts of a plant when they are talking to one other.

Page 13 Activity 2

a Learners should be able to locate the stem, leaves, flowers (if in season) and roots on each plant.

b Encourage learners to say, *These plants are the same/similar because…* and *These plants are different because …*

c Focus their attention on leaves, flowers, stem, tree trunk and bark, size, colour, texture, etc.

d Focus on the fact that big plants (including trees) have a stem, leaves, flowers and roots.

e Focus on the fact that small plants (including grass) also have a stem, leaves, flowers and roots.

Further activities

- Ask learners to complete Workbook page 7: Plant parts.

- Extend learning by focusing on other parts of plants. Encourage learners to use and remember the names of other parts of plants, such as buds and leaf veins.

- Ask learners to draw a giant plant on the playground surface and use chalk to label the parts of their plant. Encourage them to check their spellings.

- Ask learners to complete the Unit 1 digital resource interactive activity: Young gardeners. Challenge learners to drag labels to the correct places on the picture of a plant.

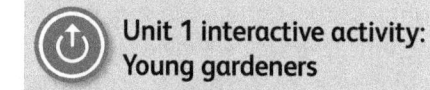 **Unit 1 interactive activity: Young gardeners**

- Using materials such as twigs, stones and leaves, ask learners to make a picture of one of the plants on the playground surface. They should also label the parts of the plant. Encourage them to check their spellings.

- Give learners copies of the Unit 1 digital resource PCM2: Parts of a plant. Ask them to cut out the sections and put them in order to create a labelled plant diagram.

 Unit 1 PCM2: Parts of a plant

Answers to PCM2:
From top to bottom: flower, stem, leaves, roots.

Success criteria

While completing the activities, assess and record learners who can:

- name the parts of a plant (stem, flowers, leaves and roots)

- answer questions about what plants look like through observation, using a hand lens or digital microscope

- explore and observe plants and collect observations, through drawings, photographs or videos, to answer questions

- make comparisons between different plants.

Workbook answers

Page 7 Plant parts

1

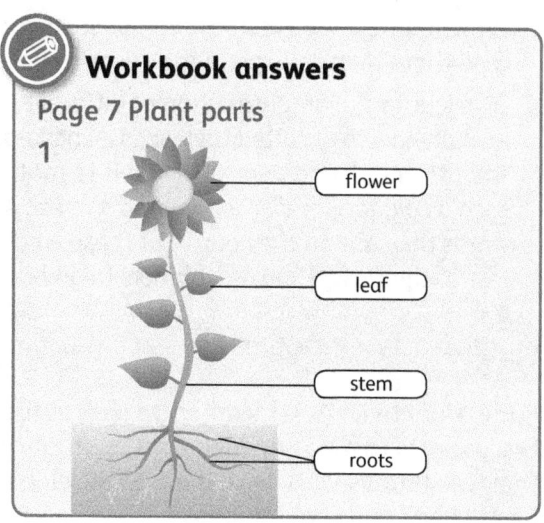

flower

leaf

stem

roots

Make a plant hunt wristband

 Learner's Book
pages 14–15

 Digital Resource

Objectives

- Know that plants are living things. (1Bp1)
- Try to answer questions by collecting evidence through observation. (1Ep1)
- Name the major parts of a plant, looking at real plants and models. (1Bp4)
- Explore and observe in order to collect evidence (measurements and observations) to answer questions. (1Eo1)
- Suggest ideas and follow instructions. (1Eo2)

Background information

The aims of the activities on page 14 of the Learner's Book are to consolidate learners' knowledge of plant parts and their names as they make a plant wristband. As part of the activities, they follow pictorial and written instructions to make their wristband. They are then able to suggest ideas for what to put onto it and what pattern to make.

The purpose of the activities on page 15 of the Learner's Book is to introduce learners to ideas about seeds. All flowering plants produce seeds. Seeds do not need light to germinate or start growing. This is because the seeds have their own food store, which is protected by a hard outer coat. The aim of the parent plant is to make sure that the seeds are dispersed so that they do not grow close to the plant. This ensures that the new plants will grow well. Seeds need water, air and the correct temperature for that type of seed.

Seeds vary depending on the parent plants. Some are very small, such as orchid, sesame, caraway and poppy seeds. Others are very large, such as palm and coconut tree seeds. One of the key aims of these activities is for learners to know that seeds come in different shapes, sizes and colours, as well as that all of them could, given suitable conditions, germinate.

Be careful

- Some learners are allergic to seeds, such as sunflower seeds, as well as to nuts.

Starter activity suggestions

- Take the class outdoors to look for different parts of plants that they can use to stick onto their wristbands. You could give learners cards which tell them which parts they can use, such as stem and flower, or leaf and flowers. Alternatively, give them a selection of colours to match, such as shades of green, yellow, red and purple.

- Give learners hand lenses or digital microscopes and a selection of seeds to choose from. You could include, for example, haricot, kidney, mung or soya beans, lentils, maize, wheat, dried peas, orange, apple and melon seeds, as well as onion, lettuce and radish seeds. Do not put too many seeds out at first, as some learners will flit from seed to seed, rather than looking at one or two different seeds in detail. Give them time to explore the seeds to note similarities and differences between them.

- Give learners a larger selection of different seeds. Ask them to sort their seeds into groups. Ask them to explain how they sorted their seeds. Encourage the use of scientific vocabulary relating to textures, such as *smooth*, *rough* and *bumpy*. Link this to mathematics, for example, shape and size, by letting them use words such as *bigger*, *smaller*, *longer* and *shorter*. As you listen to learners, celebrate their vocabulary by writing the words they use on the board. For those who can, allow them to write their own words. Share this list with the rest of the class. Then ask learners to go back and sort the seeds again, using some of these words.

Activity notes and answers

Page 14 Activity 1 Ask learners to look at the picture and suggest how they could make the wristband. Discuss how to measure their wrists so that the band fits. Then let learners support each other in making their wristbands. This helps them to develop independence and give them the opportunity to follow instructions and suggest ideas.

Page 14 Activity 2 Learners should collect a range of plant parts and decide which they are going to stick onto their wristbands. If learners have been given specific tasks, such as collecting specific parts or specific colours to match, check their progress. Give learners access to cameras to record the activity. The images could be stuck into books, with sentences describing the parts of plants used.

Page 14 Challenge yourself! Ask learners to think about which parts of the plant they have already put on their wristband and what other parts they could find. For example, if they have one kind of petal, could they find another?

Seeds

 Activity notes and answers

Page 15 Activity 1 Give learners time to explore the different fruit, cutting them open, drawing what they see first, then taking out the seeds and observing them using a hand lens and drawing them. Encourage learners to draw the seeds larger than they are, so that they can draw the shape and detail. Learners could also have access to cameras, for example, to photograph seeds, such as in an orange or melon.

Be careful

- Adult supervision is needed for learners cutting fruit with a knife.

Page 15 Activity 2 Learners should be familiar with sorting, and you will already have a vocabulary list generated from starter activities. Ask learners to look at the list and use it to sort the seeds from the fruits they have on their table.

Further activities

- Ask learners to complete Workbook page 8: Vegetables.
- Display the Unit 1 digital resource slideshow, slide 5: Seeds. Ask learners to compare the seeds in the photographs to the seeds they have sorted.
- Give groups a large seed, such as a coconut or avocado pip, to compare similarities and differences between these seeds and smaller seeds.
- Weigh a coconut on balance scales. Pour other seeds in until the scale balances show how many smaller seeds equal one coconut.
- Let learners collects seeds from food they eat at home, such as melon or pumpkin seeds. They can then dry them out to use in making seed collages.

 Unit 1 slideshow, slide 5: Seeds

Answers to slide 5:
a Listen to learners' responses. Correct any misconceptions.
b The coco de mer is the seed of the palm tree and is the largest seed in the world. The coconut is also a large seed. The wheat seeds are small seeds.
c Accept any reasonable answers, such as: *A big plant because of the size of the seed; small plants make small seeds.*

Success criteria

While completing the activities, assess and record learners who can:
- say that plants are living things
- find a range of different plants in their school grounds and collect different parts of plants
- name the parts of plants that they find
- observe the differences between seeds and sort them into different groups
- follow instructions to make their plant wristband and suggest their own ideas.

Eating parts of plants

Learner's Book
pages 16–17

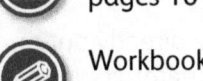

Workbook
pages 8–9

Objectives

- Know that plants need light and water to grow. (1Bp5)
- Explore how seeds grow into flowering plants. (1Bp6)
- Make comparisons. (1Eo4)
- Try to answer questions by collecting evidence through observation. (1Ep1)
- Make predictions. (1Ep3)
- Suggest ideas and follow instructions. (1Eo2)
- Record stages in work. (1Eo3)

Background information

The activities on page 16 of the Learner's Book introduce learners to the different parts of plants that humans eat. Much of what humans eat is made up of plants. Different parts of plants are edible and these parts contain important nutrients and fibre. Depending on the country in which you live, different plants will be eaten, for example:

Roots	Stems	Leaves	Flowers	Seeds
carrots	celery	lettuce	cauliflower	maize
beetroot	asparagus	spinach	broccoli	wheat
parsnip	sugar cane	cabbage	courgette	nuts
lotus	rhubarb		nasturtium	beans
radish			artichokes	peas
ginger				gram
turnip				coffee

The activities on Learner's Book page 17 give learners the opportunity to plant their own seeds and start to consider what they will need to grow.

Starter activity suggestions

- Give groups edible parts of plants. Ask them to use labels to name the different parts: stem, flower, leaf, root, shoot and seeds.
- Learners could explore the colour and texture of the different edible parts of plants. They can then draw the plant parts.
- Follow this by cutting open the parts of different edible plants so that learners can see inside. Ask them to draw what they see. They could also use the plant parts to make prints with paint.
- Have a tasting session where learners sample different parts of plants. Make sure in each case that learners know and can say which plant parts they are eating.

Be careful

- Check prior to collecting that plants are not poisonous or have spikes. Discuss with learners how to collect the edible parts of plants without damaging the plants.

 Activity notes and answers

Page 16 Activity 1
Answers:
b carrots – roots   celery – stem   cabbage – leaves   courgette – flowers   rice – seeds

Page 16 Activity 2 Make sure that learners know what this activity is about and what the words mean. Some learners might require support with the difference between some words, such as *hard* and *crunchy*. Learners could write the name and/or draw the plant in the first column.

You could provide learners with the photocopiable page: Tasting plant parts, on page 155 of this Teacher's Pack. This provides a blank copy of the table for them to complete.

Page 16 Talk partners Give learners a paper plate on which to record, either by drawing or modelling with dough, the different parts of plants that they ate.

Growing seeds

 Activity notes and answers

Page 17 Activity 1 Ensure that learners have followed the instructions to plant their seeds. Encourage them to support each other by checking what the other learner is doing, and offering advice. Ask them how they could record what they did, such as by drawing, photographing or making a video of planting seeds.

Page 17 Activity 2 Encourage learners to record their answers in a similar way to how the instructions have been laid out.

a Ask learners to think back to previous learning about what living things need to stay alive. Remind them that plants are alive. They could write words down or share ideas with their partner.

b Check their drawings. Some learners will be able to add a sentence to describe what the plants will need. Some would also benefit from being able to talk through their ideas shown in their drawings.

Further activities

- Ask learners to complete Workbook page 8: Vegetables, and Workbook page 9: Planting seeds.
- Make a salad or a soup with a group of learners. Use different plant parts and give everyone a taste.
- Create with learners a display showing plants growing, with the names of parts that are eaten.
- Take a trip to the produce section of a local grocery store or vegetable market. Let learners identify vegetables and say which part of the plant we can eat.

Success criteria

While completing the activities, assess and record learners who can:

- say that plants need light and water to grow
- plant seeds and observe plants growing
- make comparisons between different plants and parts of plants
- answer questions through observations of seeds
- make predictions by drawing what the seed will grow into
- follow instructions to plant a seed
- record by drawing, photographing or videoing planting seeds.

 Workbook answers

Page 8 Vegetables

1 yam – root
  celery – stem
  beans – seeds
  cabbage – leaves
  cauliflower – flower

2 Check learners' answers.

Page 9 Planting seeds

1 a Top left is 2 – seed being planted.
    Bottom left is 3 – soil being covered.
    Top right is 4 – seed being watered.

2 b Labels should include leaves, stem, flower; some learners might show roots.

What do seeds need to grow?

 Learner's Book
pages 18–19

 Workbook
page 10

Objectives

- Know that plants need light and water to grow. (1Bp5)
- Explore how seeds grow into flowering plants. (1Bp6)
- Try to answer questions by collecting evidence through observation. (1Ep1)
- Make predictions. (1Ep3)
- Suggest ideas and follow instructions. (1Eo2)
- Model and communicate ideas in order to share, explain and develop them. (1Eo6)

Background information

The aim of the activities on page 18 of the Learner's Book is to illustrate that seeds need water to germinate. On page 19 of the Learner's Book, the aim is for learners to observe the seeds that they have planted in Activity 1 on page 18. This will help them to learn that seeds do not need light to germinate and to observe what happens when seeds germinate.

Use the word *germinate* and scaffold learners in understanding that seeds germinate when they have water, warmth and air. They do not need soil to germinate – some will germinate on, for example, filter or blotting paper. However, growth will not be as good as if they were in a suitable soil.

These activities also introduce learners to the word *prediction*. Scaffold the word by saying, *A prediction is when we say what we think will happen.* This is more appropriate than telling learners that a prediction is a guess, as a prediction is based on using some knowledge.

On page 19 of the Learner's Book, the focus is on learners observing and recording the seed germinating and the plant growing. This will help them to understand the sequence of events and that these events are repeated in different seeds. It is also another opportunity to consolidate and apply learners' knowledge of plant parts.

Starter activity suggestions

- Remind learners of previous activities about what is alive or not alive. Ask them if plants are alive and how they know they are. Use this to elicit what they know about life processes and how these apply to humans and to plants.
- Discuss the two statements in Activity 1 on Learner's Book page 18. Ask learners to talk in their groups about which they agree or disagree with, and why.
- Ask learners to predict which seeds will grow: those with water or those without, giving reasons for their prediction. Give each learner one vote each and ask them to vote according to their prediction. They could write a number on their individual whiteboards (for example, 1 – with water, 2 – without water) and hold them up for you to record on the board, either as numbers or a simple pictograph. Refer back to this once the plants have grown. Ask learners if their predictions were correct.
- Discuss with learners what they are expected to do, using the instructions on page 18. This is a comparative test where learners compare watering with not watering. Ask learners to think about whether or not both pots should be placed in the same place or in different places. This will elicit early ideas about fair testing, even though, at this stage, learners are not expected to carry out fair tests.

Activity notes and answers

Talk partners Listen to partners discussing whether they had decided to water the seeds or not. Observe if the learners' discussions led them to recognising that seeds need water to grow.

Page 18 Activity 1 For learners to be able to observe this, it will be better if they use transparent plastic containers, such as plastic cups or cut-down plastic bottles. Explain that they will need to plant the seed between the soil and the edge of the container. They will then be able to observe the seed germinating. Check that learners have followed the instructions, planting seeds in two different pots and watering one and not the other.

Answers:

b Check learners' predictions. Ask them to give reasons for their predictions.

c Support those learners who are unsure of what to write as their prediction.

How do seeds grow?

 Activity notes and answers

Page 19 Talk partners

a Listen to partners discussing predictions about what happens when a seed germinates and a plant grows. This will help to you find out if they know that a seed grows into a plant.

b Check learners' drawings. Encourage them to label the plant parts.

 ICT links

Show learners a time-lapse video clip from the internet of a seed germinating in slow motion. Freeze-frame at set points which show, for example, the shoot and roots, first leaves, and so on. Discuss what learners observe.

Further activities

- Ask learners to complete Workbook page 10: What do seeds need?

- Take the class outside, or use a large indoor space, such as the hall. Ask learners to role-play being a seed which is growing into a plant. Give them the opportunity to show their growing sequence to someone else. Ask them to tell the person they observed what they noticed, such as shoot, roots, stem, leaves and even flowers.

- Bring learners together to role-play being, for example, watercress seeds sprinkled on the ground, germinating and growing.

Success criteria

While completing the activities, assess and record learners who can:

- say that plants need light and water to grow
- plant seeds and observe plants growing
- answer questions through observations of seeds
- make predictions by drawing what the seed will grow into
- follow instructions to plant a seed
- model and communicate seeds germinating and growing into plants through role play.

 Workbook answers

Page 10 What do seeds need?

1 Accept pictures that show appropriate ideas, such as planting two sets of seeds and watering one and not watering the other.

2 For example, *I think that the seeds that are watered will grow/germinate.*
I think that the seeds that are not watered will not grow/germinate.

Observe how a seed grows

 Learner's Book pages 20–21

 Workbook page 11

 Digital Resource

Objectives

- Know that plants need light and water to grow. (1Bp5)
- Try to answer questions by collecting evidence through observation. (1Ep1)
- Ask questions and contribute to discussions about how to seek answers. (1Ep2)
- Make predictions. (1Ep3)
- Decide what to do to try to answer a science question. (1Ep4)
- Record stages in work. (1Eo3)
- Make comparisons. (1Eo4)
- Compare what happened with predictions. (1Eo5)

Background information

The aims of the activities on pages 20 and 21 of the Learner's Book are to apply and further develop knowledge of plant growth, while also focusing on developing scientific enquiry skills. The activities on page 20 of the Learner's Book also let learners engage in activities that require them to do observations over time.

The expectation is that learners will know from previous activities that plants need water to grow. Learners observe plant growth over time and record their observations by drawing what they see and annotating pictures. Some seeds germinate more quickly than others and plant growth is faster. Therefore, some observations need to be recorded on a daily basis; others can be recorded less regularly because changes take place more slowly.

Choose fast-germinating and growing seeds, such as beans. Watercress seeds would be suitable for the activity on page 21. They will change during the course of one week.

The activities on page 21 of the Learner's Book let learners engage in developing scientific enquiry skills linked to carrying out a simple comparative test. Learners answer the question, *When plants are above the soil, do they need light to grow?* They do this by carrying out a comparative test, placing one plant in light and another in darkness. The question is specific to reinforce the idea that seeds do not need light to grow, but the plant above ground with leaves does.

Starter activity suggestions

- Show a time-lapse video clip from the internet of a seed germinating and growing into a sunflower. Stop the clip at appropriate points. Ask learners to describe what has been happening. Encourage them to use correct scientific vocabulary.

- Give learners large sheets of paper folded into sections. Stop the video clip at appropriate points and ask learners to draw what they see. The aim of this is to practise recording plant growth. This will help them understand how to record this in Activity 2 on page 20 and Activity 1 on page 21.

- Discuss with learners what the picture on page 21 shows. Ask partners to talk about what they think they have to do and why. Listen to their conversations to check that they know how to set up their activity. Help them to create their diary, which could be in the form of a mini-book.

 ### Activity notes and answers

Page 20 Activity 1 The instructions tell learners to plant the seeds next to the side of the container. This ensures that they can observe the seed as it germinates. Check that learners follow the instructions correctly.

Page 20 Activity 2 Check that learners complete their diary entries and that they label the parts of the plant. Some learners will be able to write a sentence to describe the changes.

Do plants need light to grow?

 Activity notes and answers

Page 21 Activity 1 Ask learners to predict what they think will happen to each plant. You could ask them to draw and write a sentence to record their predictions. They can then compare what happened with their predictions.

Encourage learners to work independently in pairs. Give them specific times during the day to check their plants, discuss changes, record observations and water plants. Remind them to focus on the changes, as well as the similarities and differences between the two plants. The aims are for learners to describe the differences between plants grown in light and dark, and to record their observations in a simple chart.

Check learners' predictions, diary entries and their final comparison of what happened to their predictions. Ask learners what they think they have learnt from the activity, such as that plants need light to grow well.

Page 21 Talk partners Encourage them to reflect on previous activities and how they can use their experience of growing plants to find out if all plants need light to keep growing.

Further activities

- Ask learners to complete Workbook page 11: What do plants need?
- As a class activity, discuss the results of growing plants in light and no light. List the similarities and differences. Support learners in talking about the changes over time and in making comparisons.
- As a whole class activity, discuss what happened to the plants. Compare this to learners' predictions. Support learners in saying what they have learnt about growing plants and writing down what they know.
- Show learners the Unit 1 digital resource video clip: Bean seed germination.
- Display the Unit 1 digital resource slideshow, slide 6: What have you learnt about seeds and growing plants? Use the questions to find out if learners can apply what they know about plant growth to the context of growing watercress.

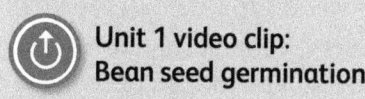 **Unit 1 video clip: Bean seed germination**

 Unit 1 slideshow, slide 6: What have you learnt about seeds and growing plants?

Answers to slide 6:
a No
b Accept any reasonable answers, for example, *Put seeds in some soil in a container; watered it; gave it warmth and light.*
c Answers could include, for example, *The watercress might wilt; it might die.*
d Answers could include *yellow, wilted, stringy.*

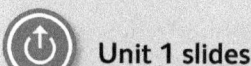 **Success criteria**

While completing the activities, assess and record learners who can:

- know that plants need light and water to grow
- answer questions by observing how plants grow
- ask questions about plants and talk about how to answer them
- predict what will happen to the plants
- decide how to answer questions about plants
- record observations of plants growing
- make comparisons between plants
- compare what happened to plants with their predictions.

Workbook answers

Page 11 What do plants need?
1 a Check that learners' drawings are appropriate for answering the question (*Do plants need light to grow?*). For example, they could draw one plant in a cupboard and one in a sunny place.
 b For example: plant seeds; place one set in darkness and the other in light; water both the same; check seeds to see what is happening.
2 Teacher to check learners' predictions.

Measuring plants growing

 Learner's Book
pages 22–23

 Workbook
page 12

 Digital Resource

Objectives

- Explore ways that different animals and plants inhabit local environments. (1Bp3)
- Explore how seeds grow into flowering plants. (1Bp6)
- Try to answer questions by collecting evidence through observation. (1Ep1)
- Explore and observe in order to collect evidence (measurements and observations) to answer questions. (1Eo1)
- Record stages in work. (1Eo3)
- Make comparisons. (1Eo4)

Background information

The purpose of the activities on page 22 of the Learner's Book is to introduce learners to non-standard measurements by using apparatus such as cubes. When done on a daily basis to measure plants growing, the results can be put together to form a simple graph that shows how a plant grows. Learners can then calculate how much taller plants grow from day to day by counting the additional cubes.

Measurement is important. It provides numbers, which is data that we can analyse and use for drawing conclusions. For example, *On day 6 the plant was 7 cubes tall. On day 9 it was 10 cubes tall, so the plant has grown by 3 cubes.* Such experiences lay the foundation for generating and handling data in later stages.

The activities on Learner's Book page 23 continue to develop learners' knowledge about where plants grow and the idea that plants grow in different places.

Starter activity suggestions

- Let learners practise measuring one of their own plants by using cubes. Ask them to decide where they should measure the cubes from, such as from the base of the plant pot or from the base of the plant.
- Show learners four to six plants (of different heights, if possible), measured with cubes next to them. Ask a series of questions, such as: *Which plant is the tallest or the shortest?*
- Display the Unit 1 digital resource slideshow, slide 7: A plant's growth. Use it to illustrate what a graph looks like and to engage learners in questions about the graph and plant growth.

 Unit 1 slideshow, slide 7: A plant's growth

Answers to slide 7:
a 1 block
b 20 blocks
c Day 9
d The plant needed food, light and water.

 Activity notes and answers

Page 22 Activity 1 A number of the activities in this unit use cubes for measuring plants. This is the beginning of using non-standard measurement. Make sure that learners use cubes that are not so small that learners find it difficult to count them, or that the numbers are outside their counting range.
a 6 cubes   b 15 cubes   c 5 cubes

Plants live in different places

 Activity notes and answers

Page 23 Talk partners Encourage learners to think about areas where they have seen plants growing in the school grounds, locally, around their home and when they have been on holiday.

Further activities

- Ask learners to complete Workbook page 12: Measuring bean plants.
- Provide learners with simple identification cards, books or pages relating to the plants in the school grounds. Ask them to name some plants.
- When learners are outdoors looking for plants, ask them to decide whether the plant they are standing next to is shorter/taller and wider/narrower than they are themselves. This helps to develop their use of comparative measurements in science.

Success criteria

While completing the activities, assess and record learners who can:
- find out where plants live
- know that plants need light and water to grow
- find out how seeds grow into plants
- think of ways to answer questions through observing plants grow
- measure plants to answer questions
- use a diary to record plants growing
- compare plants growing
- compare with themselves how tall, short, wide and narrow plants are.

 Workbook answers

Page 12 Measuring bean plants
1 a 6 cubes
   b 8 cubes
   c Day 9
   d Day 1

Plant detectives

 Learner's Book
pages 24–25

 Workbook
pages 13–14

Objectives

- Explore ways that different animals and plants inhabit local environments. (1Bp3)
- Explore and observe in order to collect evidence (measurements and observations) to answer questions. (1Eo1)
- Record stages in work. (1Eo3)
- Make comparisons. (1Eo4)
- Model and communicate ideas in order to share, explain and develop them. (1Eo6)

Background information

The purpose of the activities on page 24 of the Learner's Book is to consolidate the idea that plants are living things and that they grow in different places in the school grounds or the local environment. Encourage identification and naming of plants by giving learners identification charts to match pictures of the plants, their flowers, leaves, and so on. Learners enjoy learning names of plants and such activities help to develop observational skills. Focus learners' attention on the different parts of plants, thereby helping to consolidate learning. At the same time, you can use it as an assessment of what they have learnt.

The purpose of the activity on page 25 of the Learner's Book is to consolidate learners' knowledge. It offers an assessment opportunity of parts of a plant through making a model plant. Discuss with learners the idea that a model represents a real thing, like a plant. Explain that scientists often use models. The idea is to be as accurate/correct as they can be in showing what a plant looks like.

Starter activity suggestions

- Take the class outdoors to look for plants in the school grounds or local environment. If possible, give pairs a camera so that they can take photographs of, for example:
  - different plants
  - different places where plants are growing
  - parts of a plant.
- Develop learners' ability to choose the best photographs and delete others. Tell them that at the end they have to choose, for example, their six best photographs to keep.
- Give groups different things to look for, such as matching leaf shapes, matching colours, and biggest and smallest leaves. Encourage them to look for plants in unusual places.
- Give learners simple identification charts to use to find the names of common plants in the school grounds or local environment.

Activity notes and answers

Page 24 Activity 1 Talk with groups, asking them what they found, where, and what they noticed about the plant. Ask about plant parts they can see and comparisons between plants, such as *tallest/shortest*. Engage learners in discussions about where plants are growing, to help secure their understanding of plants growing in different places. Also challenge learners to think about where plants get light and water from to live.

Page 24 Activity 2
a Some learners will find many different plants and enjoy naming them if simple identification cards are available. Focus their attention the size of the plant, where it was found, what it looks like, leaves, flowers and so on.
b Give learners a clipboard and pencil or a sketch book so that if they want to, they can draw plants. Some learners will find it easier to take photographs.

Page 24 Talk partners Encourage learners to share what they have found, focusing on similarities and differences between plants. Ask learners to say where they found the plants. For example, if they found similar plants, were they in the same place; did they notice if it was sunny, shady or between rocks?

Page 24 Challenge yourself! This challenge develops learners' understanding that there are many shades of green in plants. Before they start collecting leaves, explain that when collecting leaves from people's gardens or from public parks, they should first ask for permission. Certain endangered plants are protected and may not be picked.

Making a model plant

 Activity notes and answers

Page 25 Activity 1 Check the plant models that learners make. Ask them to label the plant parts and show their plant to someone else in the class.

Page 25 Talk partners The first time this is done, it may help learners if they share ideas before they start of what they might be looking for, such as correct parts of the plant in the right place. Then they can give more accurate feedback about their partner's model.

Further activities

- Ask learners to complete Workbook page 13: Plant detectives, and page 14: Design a plant model.

- Take the class outdoors into the school grounds to measure plants. Supply some objects that learners could use for measuring, such as sticks and large blocks. Suggest that they measure using their hands. Also offer standard measures, such as rulers, metre rules and tape measures, for those who want to use them.

- When outdoors, ask learners to *estimate* which is the *tallest*, *smallest*, *narrowest* or *widest* plant, using comparative mathematics language.

- Learners could compare themselves to plants in terms of size. Give them cameras to take photographs of themselves next to plants, which they could stick in their books and write a sentence.

- Give learners the opportunity to display and share their model plant with other learners, and share what they know about their model.

Success criteria

While completing the activities, assess and record learners who can:

- find out where plants live in the school grounds
- measure plants to answer questions
- draw or take photographs of the plants they find
- compare plants growing in different places
- make a model plant to show parts of a plant.

 Workbook answers

Page 13 Plant detectives

1 a Check the three plants that learners draw.
  b Check the sentences about where the plants were found, for example, soil, crack in ground, wall.
2 Check that learners have labelled the stem, leaf, flower on each plant. Some learners might show where the roots are.

Page 14 Make a model plant

1 a Learners draw a design of their model.
  b Learners choose from clean junk materials.
  c Learners should label the stem, leaves, flower and roots.
2 Encourage learners to be kind and helpful in their suggestions.

Save the plant

 Learner's Book
pages 26–27

 Workbook
page 15

 Digital Resource

Objectives

- Know that plants are living things. (1Bp1)
- Name the major parts of a plant, looking at real plants and models. (1Bp4)
- Know that plants need light and water to grow. (1Bp5)

Background information

The aim of the activity on page 26 of the Learner's Book is to elicit what learners know from this unit. As learners work, talk with them about what they know about plants, such as how they know that plants are living things, what the parts of a plant are, and what plants need to stay alive. Challenge them to use scientific vocabulary and to spell the words correctly.

The aim of the activity on page 27 of the Learner's Book is also to elicit what learners know from this unit. The flower could be created as a class activity. Make a large flower as part of a wall display onto which you write what learners know, perhaps as statements beginning, for example, with: *Anna knows that…* to provide evidence for assessment.

Starter activity suggestions

- Bring into the classroom a plant that has not been watered recently and is wilting, or one that has also been kept in the dark so that it has a yellow tinge. Use this as a starter for discussions with learners about what they think about the plant. For example, ask: *Does the plant look healthy? How do you know? What do you think the plant needs?*
- Display the Unit 1 digital resource slideshow, slide 6: What have you learnt about seeds and growing plants? Use it to revisit ideas about plant growth and to assess if learners can apply their understanding of plant growth to watercress. Go through the unit with learners, looking at pages or go through their work in books or folders.
- Pick out new words and place them on display for the learners to use in the activity on page 26. Ask them to tell you what they remember, what they found the most interesting, what they still find hard or do not understand.
- Scaffold learners into making oral and/or written statements for the activity on page 27, by offering sentence 'openers' such as: *I know that…; I can remember…; I still don't know…; I can spell…*

 Unit 1 slideshow, slide 6: What have you learnt about seeds and growing plants?

Activity notes and answers

Page 26 Activity 1
Answers:
a The plant needs water and light.
b Pictures should show the plant in light and being watered.

Page 26 Activity 2
a Provide large pieces of paper for learners to draw their plant on. Check that their drawings are appropriate.
b and c Check the words that learners have picked out from the unit. These might include, for example, stem, flower, roots, leaf.

What have you learnt about plants?

 Activity notes and answers

Page 27 Activity 1

a Encourage learners to draw a flower with large petals, with enough room to write sentences in the petals.

b Check the statements that learners write. Use this as evidence for assessment.

Further activities

• Ask learners to complete Workbook page 15: What have you learnt about plants?

• Give learners the opportunity to share what they have learnt with others in the class.

• Tell learners that they can go and read someone else's work. If they find something that they have forgotten, such as a word or a statement, they can add it to their own work.

Success criteria

While completing the activities, assess and record learners who can:

• say that plants are living things

• name parts of a plant

• say that the plant needs light and water to grow better.

 Workbook answers

Page 15 Plant words

1 Learners could work in pairs to learn to spell the words.

2 The unjumbled words are: stem, plant, leaf, tree, roots, flower.

Assessment ideas

• Ask learners to leave positive comments next to each other's work to say what they liked. This offers an early introduction to learners' peer assessing.

• Ask learners to self-assess using the 'What can you remember?' checklist on page 29 of the Learner's Book, as well as the self-assessment table on page 16 of the Workbook.

Unit 2 Ourselves

Objectives overview

Learning objective	Objective code	Learner's Book pages	Teacher's Pack pages	Workbook pages	Digital Resource Pack
Biology: Plants					
Know that there are living things and things that have never been alive.	1Bp2	28, 29	42, 43		Unit 2 slide 3
Biology: Humans and animals					
Recognise the similarities and differences between each other.	1Bh1	28, 29, 30, 31, 32, 33, 34, 37	42, 43, 44, 45, 46, 47, 48, 49, 50, 51	17, 20, 21	Unit 2 slides 3, 6, 7
Recognise and name the main external parts of the body.	1Bh2	30, 31, 33, 35, 36, 37	44, 45, 46, 47, 48, 49, 50, 51	18, 22, 23	Unit 2 slide 4, 5, 8, PCM2, interactive activity
Explore how senses enable humans and animals to be aware of the world around them.	1Bh4	36, 37, 38, 39, 40, 41, 42, 43, 44, 45, 46, 47, 48, 49, 50	50, 51, 52, 53, 54, 55, 56, 57, 58, 59, 60, 61, 62, 63	22, 23, 24, 25, 27, 28, 29, 30	Unit 2 slide 8, video clip
Scientific enquiry: Ideas and evidence					
Try to answer questions by collecting evidence through observation.	1Ep1	30, 31, 32, 33, 34, 35, 40, 41	44, 45, 46, 47, 48, 49, 54, 55	17, 20, 21, 25	Unit 2 slide 7
Scientific enquiry: Plan investigative work					
Ask questions and contribute to discussions about how to seek answers.	1Ep2			29	
Make predictions.	1Ep3	29, 32, 43, 45	42, 43, 46 47, 56, 57, 58, 59		
Decide what to do to try to answer a science question.	1Ep4	31, 34, 46, 48, 49	44, 45, 48, 49, 60, 61, 62, 63	26	

Learning objective	Objective code	Learner's Book pages	Teacher's Pack pages	Workbook pages	Digital Resource Pack
Scientific enquiry: Obtain and present evidence					
Explore and observe in order to collect evidence (measurements and observations) to answer questions.	1Eo1	30, 31, 32, 33, 34, 40, 41	44, 45, 46, 47, 48, 49, 54, 55	17, 19, 20, 21, 26, 27, 28	Unit 2 slide 6
Suggest ideas and follow instructions.	1Eo2	38, 39, 42, 43, 45, 46, 47, 48, 49	52, 53, 56, 57, 58, 59, 60, 61, 62, 63	26	
Record stages in work.	1Eo3	40, 41, 42, 43, 45, 46, 47, 49	54, 55, 56, 57, 58, 59, 60, 61, 62, 63		
Scientific enquiry: Consider evidence and approach					
Make comparisons.	1Eo4	29, 31, 32, 33, 34, 36, 37, 38, 39, 40, 41, 42, 44, 45, 46, 47, 48, 49	42, 43, 44, 45, 46, 47, 48, 49, 50, 51, 52, 53, 54, 55, 56, 57, 58, 59, 60, 61, 62, 63	17, 20, 21, 24, 25, 26, 27, 29	Unit 2 slides 3, 8
Compare what happened with predictions.	1Eo5	32, 38, 42, 43, 45, 46, 47	46, 47, 52, 53, 56, 57, 58, 59, 60, 61		
Model and communicate ideas in order to share, explain and develop them.	1Eo6	48	62, 63		PCM1

All about me!

 Learner's Book
pages 28–29

 Workbook
page 17

 Digital Resource

Objectives

- Know that there are living things and things that have never been alive. (1Bp2)
- Recognise the similarities and differences between each other. (1Bh1)
- Make predictions. (1Ep3)
- Make comparisons. (1Eo4)

Background information

The aim of the activities on page 28 of the Learner's Book is to elicit learners' ideas about how they know that they are alive, based on five of the life processes (eat, move, grow, sense things and breathe). The other two life processes (excrete and reproduce) are developed in later stages of the *Hodder Cambridge Primary Science* series. All these processes are needed to demonstrate being alive.

Throughout this unit, learners will be finding out about themselves. Activity 1 on page 28 suggests that they create a personal book to record what they find out about themselves. Learners could put their work from this unit into their book. The activities on page 29 of the Learner's Book focus on the idea that humans are the same yet different.

Starter activity suggestions

- Ask learners to say how they know that they are alive. Accept comments such as: *Because I can smile and run.* Alongside their ideas, develop their understanding that they are alive because they eat, grow, move, sense things and breathe.
- Working in pairs, ask learners to mime something that shows they are alive, such as breathing or growing. Their partner must work out what it is.
- Display the Unit 2 digital resource slideshow, slide 3: The same and different. Ask learners to compare the children in the slide by naming similarities and differences between the children in the photographs.

 Unit 2 slideshow, slide 3: The same and different

Answers to slide 3:
At this stage, accept anything that learners observe as a similarity or difference. Gradually bring the conversation round to the idea that similarities include features such as having a head, arms, hair and eyes, with differences linked to these features, such as different colour hair and eyes.

- Give learners mirrors so that they can look at their faces. They should note skin, hair and eye colour, shape of eyes, whether they have freckles, straight or curly hair, and so on.
- Encourage learners to stand next to each other to see if they are the same height or different. Let them compare shoe sizes and put their hands against each other to compare sizes.
- When engaging in activities where learners are comparing themselves to others, emphasise that although we are different in some ways, these differences do not make us less important than others. Make sure that learners do not use observations about differences as reasons for bullying other learners, or discriminating against them.

 Activity notes and answers

Page 28 Talk partners Listen to talk partners, and share some of their ideas with the rest of the class. At this stage, accept all answers to elicit how they know that they are living things and what they do to stay alive. Provide scaffolding by referring them to the text next to each illustration, to draw their attention to the key ideas.

Page 28 Activity 1 Check that learners have written their name correctly. Encourage learners to personalise their book by bringing photographs of themselves and their families or drawing pictures.

Page 28 Activity 2 Discuss what learners draw to show that they are alive. Check that they know what this means.

Same, similar and different

 Activity notes and answers

Page 29 Activity 1 Check that learners have copied and completed the sentences. (You might need to provide a word bank to support learners, such as hair and eye colours, and preferred foods or animals.) Give learners the photocopiable page: All about me, on page 156 of this Teacher's Pack to support this activity.

Page 29 Talk partners Listen to learners comparing similarities between themselves, such as physical attributes (for example, hair and eye colour), height or games they like to play. Then listen to learners comparing similarities and differences between themselves. They could talk about shoe size, where they live, how many brothers or sisters they have, and so on. Share some of their ideas with the class.

Further activities

- Ask learners to complete Workbook page 17: We are the same and different.
- Ask learners to complete the Unit 2 digital resource PCM1: All about me.
- Introduce the term *predict*. For example, ask: *Predict who will wear bigger shoes than you.* Ask them to explain why. For example, they may say that the person is bigger, so they think the feet will be bigger.

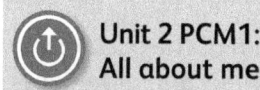
Unit 2 PCM1: All about me

 ICT links

Make a video of the whole class showing that they are alive. For example, show them moving, pretending to grow, eating and all taking a deep breath. Each time they do an action, they could say, for example, *We know we are alive because we can MOVE*.

Success criteria

While completing the activities, assess and record learners who can:
- say that they are alive and how they know that they are
- talk about the similarities and differences between themselves and someone else
- make predictions about who is taller or has bigger feet or hands than themselves
- make comparisons between each other in what they look like and what they do.

Assessment ideas

Ask learners to draw two pictures: one of themselves and the other of a family member or a friend. They must then draw two lines linking two things between them that are the same (such as hair colour) and two things that are different (such as height or clothes).

 Workbook answers

Page 17 We are the same and different

1 Check learners' drawings.

2 a Check that learners have put a small red cross next to three things that are the same on themselves and their friend.

  b Check that learners have put a small blue cross next to three things that are different on themselves and their friend.

On the outside

 Learner's Book
pages 30–31

 Workbook
page 18

 Digital Resource

Objectives

- Recognise the similarities and differences between each other. (1Bh1)
- Recognise and name the main external parts of the body. (1Bh2)
- Try to answer questions by collecting evidence through observation. (1Ep1)
- Explore and observe in order to collect evidence (measurements and observations) to answer questions. (1Eo1)
- Make comparisons. (1Eo4)
- Decide what to do to try to answer a science question. (1Ep4)

Background information

The aims of the activities on page 30 of the Learner's Book are to support learners in knowing the names of different parts of the body and how to spell the names of these parts. Mastering scientific language is about knowing key vocabulary: what each word means and how to spell the words. This will ensure that learners can communicate, using appropriate scientific words, orally and in written work. This is the reason why science words are included throughout the units.

The aim of the activities on page 31 of the Learner's Book is to reinforce learners' ability to recognise similarities and differences by comparing themselves with others. The activities also develop learners' ability to compare by using measurement – in this context, by using string for comparative measures of height. Once again language is key, focusing on words such as *height, tall, taller* and *tallest,* as well as *shorter* and *shortest.* Comparative language is key to science, so every opportunity should be taken to practise these words.

Starter activity suggestions

- Focus on the names of the body parts indicated on the page. Engage learners in fun games, such as 'Simon says'. For example, *Simon says touch your...*
- Display the Unit 2 digital resource slideshow, slide 4: Parts of the body. Use it to play a fun game to help learners remember the names of parts of the body. The answers will appear when you click on slide 5.

 Unit 2 slideshow, slide 4: Parts of the body

- Play 'Spot the difference'. Tell learners to look at their partner while you count to 10 or 15. Tell them that during that time, they have to spot as many differences as they can and then share them with each other.
- Ask learners to complete the interactive activity: Who am I? In this activity they label different body parts.

 Unit 2 interactive activity: Who am I?

Activity notes and answers

Page 30 Talk partners Check that learners know the correct names for different parts of the body.

Page 30 Activity 1 Check that learners have located and labelled parts of the body correctly.

Page 30 Activity 2 Check that learners can spell words correctly. If any of the learners can already spell the words, extend the list to words such as shoulder and ankle. Alternatively, ask them to choose words (related to the body) that they don't already know to learn.

Spotting differences and similarities

 Activity notes and answers

Page 31 Talk Partners (1) Listen to learners sharing similarities and differences about the people in the photograph. Prompt them if they have difficulty using questions such as: *Are they all the same age or height? Do they all have the same colour hair?*

Page 31 Talk Partners (2) Learners might suggest:

a My partner is different because we have different colour eyes, hair, different height and shoe size.

b Learners could suggest height, shoe size, clothes, hair, eyes, skin, ears, nose, mouth, size of hands.

c Learners could suggest height, shoe size, clothes, hair, eyes, skin, ears, nose, mouth, size of hands.

Page 31 Activity 1 Check that learners have used the string correctly to measure each other's height, and have compared strings to find out who is the tallest. Check that they have completed the sentence correctly.

Further activities

- Ask learners to complete Workbook page 18: Parts of the body.

- Ask learners to choose key science words that they are unsure of how to spell. Write them on a card for learners to learn as a home-school activity.

- Ask learners to complete the Unit 2 digital resource PCM2: Parts of the body.

- Play 'Simon says spell', with you or a learner pointing to a part of the body to be spelled out.

- Use the string from each learner to create a height bar graph, either on the wall or floor area. Tell learners to organise themselves in height order, by using their string and comparing it with those of the other learners. Then they stick their string (in height order) onto the wall or floor with tape or sticky tack, with a label on or above with their name.

Success criteria

While completing the activities, assess and record learners who can:

- name similarities and differences between themselves and their partner
- name different parts of their body
- answer questions by observing similarities and differences
- answer questions by measuring each other
- compare similarities and differences between each other
- say what they will do to answer a question.

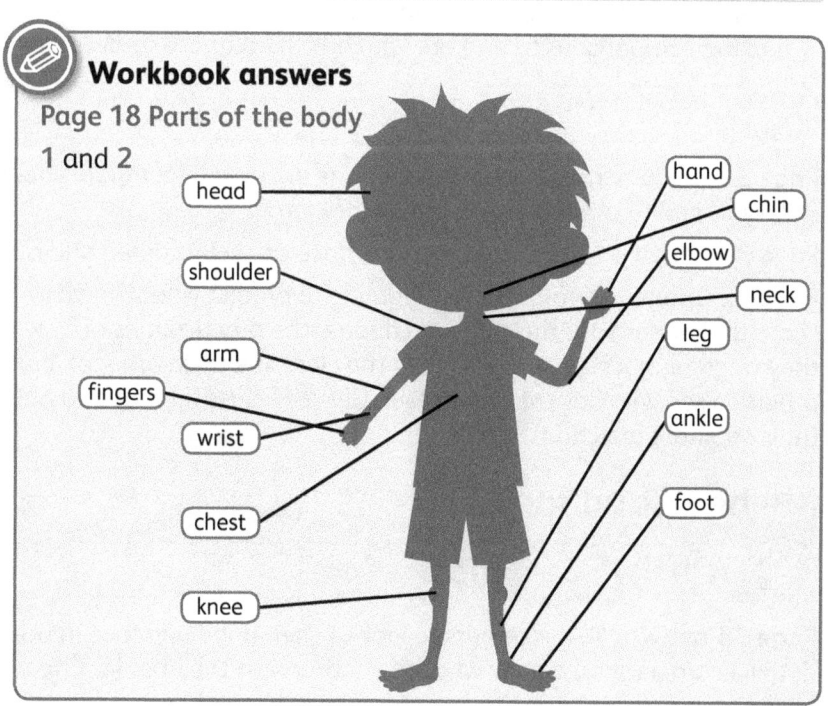

Unit 2 PCM2: Parts of the body

Answers to PCM2:

knee, foot, ankle, arm, shoulder, finger, wrist, neck

Workbook answers

Page 18 Parts of the body

1 and 2

head, shoulder, arm, fingers, wrist, chest, knee, hand, chin, elbow, neck, leg, ankle, foot

Shoe sizes

Learner's Book
pages 32–33

Workbook
page 19

Digital Resource

Objectives

- Recognise the similarities and differences between each other. (1Bh1)
- Recognise and name the main external parts of the body. (1Bh2)
- Try to answer questions by collecting evidence through observation. (1Ep1)
- Make predictions. (1Ep3)
- Explore and observe, in order to collect evidence (measurements and observations) to answer questions. (1Eo1)
- Make comparisons. (1Eo4)
- Compare what happened with predictions. (1Eo5)

Background information

The aims of the activities on page 32 of the Learner's Book are to develop learners' ability to make comparisons between humans, and in using non-standard measurements to find answers to questions. Provide scaffolding by asking learners to share ideas about how they could compare shoe sizes, and how they could find out if the tallest person has the biggest foot size. Give learners time to discuss this with talk partners or in small groups. Listen to their suggestions; do not discard any at this point, to develop their confidence in sharing ideas. Let learners try out their ideas. Then they should decide whether what they did was the best way to find out the answer, or whether they should try something else.

The activities on page 32 of the Learner's Book focus on recognising similarities and differences by letting learners compare their heads and faces with each other.

Starter activity suggestions

- Give learners a collection of different kinds of shoes (include adult shoes). Ask them to put the shoes in order from the smallest to the biggest size. Allow learners to choose their own approach. For example, they might look inside the shoe for the size number, or put shoes next to each other to find out which is bigger/smaller.
- Ask learners to draw around their own feet or shoes on paper. They should then cut out the shapes and place them next to those of their talk partner to find out who has the biggest/smallest feet.
- Extend the previous activity by telling partners to join with one or more pairs and repeat the activity, making comparisons to find out who has the biggest/smallest feet.

Activity notes and answers

Page 32 Talk partners Check that learners are able to compare shoes, to say if they are the same or different, and to use the words *smaller* or *bigger*.

Page 32 Activity 1 Check that learners have correctly copied and completed the sentence.

Page 32 Challenge yourself! Ask learners to predict what the answer to the question will be. Ask them to share their ideas with the class and discuss the practicalities of how they will find the answer. For example, they might suggest that everyone in the class line up in order of shoe size, or compare their shoes with others to see who has the bigger feet. Give the class time to find out and compare what they found with their original prediction.

My head and face

Activity notes and answers

Page 33 Activity 1 Ask learners to look at their head and face in the mirror. Guide them towards observing detail. Learners should draw what they observe in their books. Check that learners label different parts of the head and face, referring them to the words in the boxes on Learner's Book page 33 for help with spellings.

Page 33 Activity 2
Answers:
a and **b** Accept answers that relate to the picture their partner has drawn in comparison to their own. Encourage learners to communicate in a sentence, so that they have practised the sentence before writing it in Activity 3.

Page 33 Activity 3
Answers:
a, b and **c** Accept answers that relate to the picture their partner has drawn in comparison to their own. Make sure they have written three complete sentences, using the sentence starters provided in the Learner's Book.

Further activities

- Ask learners to complete Workbook page 19: How tall?
- Display the Unit 2 digital resource slideshow, slide 6: Tallest and shortest. Use it to show the height of children to practise simple data handling. Ask learners to use the graph to answer the questions. You might need to scaffold some learners who are unsure of the comparative words *taller, shorter, shortest* and *tallest*. Ask learners to put themselves in order, according to shoe size, from smallest to biggest. Take photographs and show them to the learners. Ask learners what they notice about the height of children going from the smallest to biggest shoe size. What is the pattern? (Explain the pattern by asking if it looks as if these heights are in the same order as the shoe sizes.)

 Unit 2 slideshow, slides 6: tallest and shortest

Answers to slide 6: a Sam   **b** Dev   **c** taller   **d** shorter   **e** shorter

- Challenge learners to use string to compare and find out, for example, who has the longest arm span or shortest hand span, or if head sizes are the same.
- Display the Unit 2 digital resource slideshow, slide 7: How do you feel? Discuss how people show emotion through their faces. Give learners time to show different emotions using their faces. They should observe their own facial expressions in mirrors before showing these facial expressions to their partners.

 Unit 2 slideshow, slide 7: How do you feel?

Answers to slide 7:
a Introduce the term 'facial expression' and accept learners' explanations of the emotions they see.

Success criteria

While completing the activities, assess and record learners who can:
- recognise the similarities and differences between each other
- label parts of the head and face
- answer questions by looking at shoe sizes
- make predictions about who has the biggest shoes
- compare measurements, such as feet, hands and arm span, to answer questions
- make comparisons between each other's shoe size and height
- say if they think someone's shoe size or height is more or less than their own, using what they have found out.

 Workbook answers
Page 19 How tall?
1 **a** Jack
   b Amir
   c Yes
   d Yes

Measure your head

Learner's Book
pages 34–35

Workbook
pages 20–21

Objectives

- Recognise the similarities and differences between each other. (1Bh1)
- Recognise and name the main external parts of the body. (1Bh2)
- Try to answer questions by collecting evidence through observation. (1Ep1)
- Decide what to do to try to answer a science question. (1Ep4)
- Explore and observe, in order to collect evidence (measurements and observations) to answer questions. (1Eo1)
- Make comparisons. (1Eo4)

Background information

The aims of the activities on page 34 of the Learner's Book are to practise and consolidate learners' ability to use non-standard measurements in science, as well as comparative language. Learners are also expected to suggest ideas about how to measure each other's heads, and then try out those ideas. Then they use their measurements (evidence) to answer the original question.

The activities on page 35 of the Learner's Book reinforce learning about parts of the face and head, and support learners in learning to read, write and spell scientific words relating to parts of the face. Apply approaches used in, for example, literacy to support spelling; the example on the Learner's Book page uses phonics. At regular intervals, check that learners not only can say words, but that they also know what the words mean and can spell them. Gradually, as learners' reading ability improves, they will be able to use and check spellings and meanings of scientific words by using the dictionary at the back of the Learner's Book. Use this dictionary with the class, so that they know where to find it and how to access a scientific dictionary.

Starter activity suggestions

- Put out a range of resources for learners to choose from to answer the question, *Is your head bigger or smaller than your partner's?* Include string, card and any other items you think might be useful. Do not tell learners how to measure their heads or what to use. This allows you to assess their problem-solving skills and to see if some learners can apply what they did in previous activities to a new situation.
- Although Stage 1 learners are only expected to use non-standard measures, do include items such as tape measures for those who want to use them, or to challenge some learners in mathematics.
- Make spelling new scientific words fun. For example, ask learners to whisper, sing and shout new words. Focus on exaggerating the phonics so that learners know the letters and consonant blends and digraphs, such as: *ch*.

Activity notes and answers

Page 34 Talk partners Listen to learners discussing and planning how to find out whether their head is bigger or smaller than their partner's. Accept any appropriate response and scaffold where necessary, including reminding them of how they have measured using string in past activities.

Page 34 Activity 1 Observe learners trying out their ideas, checking that they measure appropriately. Make sure that learners can articulate what they found out, so that they can answer the original question. Challenge them to use their evidence. Check that the answer is appropriate to the measurement: *My head is bigger/smaller than my partner's head.*

Page 34 Activity 2

a This could be done in the context of learners comparing in small groups and then joining groups together. A simple approach is for learners to place their string against the string belonging to other learners.

b Ask learners to count how many learners have bigger heads than themselves. They could do this by using a simple tally chart and making a mark each time someone has a bigger head than themselves.

c Ask learners to count how many learners have smaller heads than they have. Check that learners are placing their piece of string against their partner's piece of string carefully, beginning at one end, with both strings placed together. You might need to demonstrate this.

d Help learners to compare the lengths of their strings.

Learning new words

 Activity notes and answers

Page 35 Activity 1 Observe learners working together. Use this as an assessment to make sure that all learners can name the parts of the face.

Page 35 Activity 2 Make sure that learners can read the words in the box. Listen to learners spelling and writing the words, and check that they are correct. Check that learners practise writing and spelling words and that they are making progress. Engage learners in peer assessment, testing each other to find out if they can spell the words.

Further activities

- Ask learners to complete Workbook page 20: Comparing heads and page 21: Taller or shorter?

- Put out challenges for learners to do, such as letting learners work out if their hand span is longer or shorter than an object. The heights of different animals could be placed on a wall, so that learners can make comparisons and add their name and results to a simple class table or chart, as in the example below.

Are you taller or shorter than a kangaroo?

Name	Taller	Shorter
Jade	✓	✗

- Leave out different standard measuring equipment for learners to explore, such as rulers, tape measures, trundle wheels.

- Ask learners to say which words they still find hard to read and/or write. Help them to make spelling cards to take home to learn scientific words.

 ICT links

Learners could take a photograph to show how to measure their head. These could be labelled, or have a sentence describing what they did written underneath.

Success criteria

While completing the activities, assess and record learners who can:

- talk about the similarities and differences between each other
- say the names of parts of the face
- try to answer questions using observations comparing lengths of string
- talk about and decide how to measure each other's head
- compare the strings they have used to measure heads to answer their question
- make comparisons and say if their head is bigger or smaller than someone else's.

 Workbook answers

Page 20 Comparing heads
1 a 18 cubes b 15 cubes
   c Cheng   d Peng
   e 3 cubes

Page 21 Taller or shorter?
1 a shorter   b taller
   c taller   d taller
   e shorter
2 Check learners' sentences.

The five senses – sight

Learner's Book
pages 36–37

Workbook
page 22

Digital Resource

Objectives

- Recognise the similarities and differences between each other. (1Bh1)
- Recognise and name the main external parts of the body. (1Bh2)
- Explore how senses enable humans and animals to be aware of the world around them. (1Bh4)
- Make comparisons. (1Eo4)

Background information

The activities on pages 36 and 37 of the Learner's Book introduce the five senses and the parts of the body which are associated with these senses. Learners have learnt the names of parts of their bodies, such as nose, eyes, hands, ears and tongue. However, they might not yet connect these with the idea of the five senses. It is this link that is a key aim of the activities related to the senses. Check that basic knowledge of body parts related to the senses is secure. If it is not, clarify what learners are unsure about and use the assessment to ensure that they know those body parts. Eliciting learners' ideas at the beginning of a lesson provides you with knowledge of whether they are secure in some basic concepts before moving on.

Observational drawing is important in science. Learners need to look closely, rather than rely on what they sometimes 'think they see'. Observational drawing can make learners slow down and look at detail. This can help to consolidate learning, as well as the ability to make connections between what they observe and what they are learning. Whenever talking about any of the senses, use the word *sense*, such as *sense of smell*, *sense of taste*, to help learners to connect these words.

As learners observe the different parts of their eye, help them to understand that they can only see part of their eye. The rest of the eye is inside the head and the skull protects our eyes. Reinforce the functions (jobs) of the eyelids, eyelashes and eyebrows in terms of also protecting the eyes.

Starter activity suggestions

- Ask learners to talk about what they think the senses are. Let them share what they know, either with talk partners or small groups. Listen to their discussions to elicit what they know.
- Play a senses game. Give each pair an object, such as a lemon, lime or orange. Ask them to use their five senses (except, at this point, taste – explain that they will use taste soon). Tell them to use each of the other four senses in turn to find out about the object. Ask learners to say which part of the body they used for each sense. This helps learners to make the link between body part and sense. Collect what they have found out using four of the five senses. Link the words with the sense, such as smooth or bumpy for touch; lemony or strong for smell.
- Whichever fruit is being used, cut up pieces for learners to taste. Ask them to share what they have found out using their sense of taste.
- Learners could test each other on how to spell each of the five senses words. Tell learners that the first sense they are going to learn about is sight.
- Display the Unit 2 digital resource slideshow, slide 8: Five senses. Use it to compare the idea of humans and their five senses with other animals, and to explain why the senses are important.

Unit 2 slideshow, slide 8: Five senses

Answers to slide 8:
a Yes, we can see them use their senses.
b For example: giraffe – eyes, ears, tongue; star-nosed mole – nose; hare – ears, eyes; aye aye – ears, eyes; gorilla – hands.
c They are similar, though different shapes and sizes.

Activity notes and answers

Page 36 Talk partners: Listen to discussions and use this opportunity to assess what learners already know about the senses.

Answers:

a eyes   **b** skin   **c** ears   **d** tongue   **e** nose

Page 36 Activity 1 Check that learners are looking at the main parts of the eye shown in the diagram on the page. Ask learners what they can see and if they know any of the names of different parts of the eye.

Your eyes

 Activity notes and answers

Page 37 Activity 1 Check that learners are using their observations to describe their own eyes. You might need to suggest some shapes, such as *round*, *oval*, *big* and *small*. Check that learners know eye colours; you could show photos of different coloured eyes using Google Images or photos from magazines.

Page 37 Activity 2
Answers:

a Check drawings, making sure that learners draw a large eye. (Some learners draw it the same size as their own eye, which makes identifying parts difficult.) Make sure that they include detail.

b Check that the labels on the drawings are correct.

Page 37 Activity 3 Support learners by asking them to think about the different parts of the eye. For example, ask: *Do you have longer or shorter eyelashes than your partner? Are your eyes the same colour or the same shape?* Encourage learners to use the names of different parts of the eye.

Further activities

- Ask learners to complete Workbook page 22: Where are our senses?
- Create a large diagram of the eye as a display, with labels that learners can stick on using Velcro or sticky tak.
- Play 'I spy' games with learners, applying phonics. For example, *I spy with my little eye something beginning with …* (give the letter sound).
- Play 'How many objects can you remember?' Show learners a tray of objects. Then cover it and ask the class or group to name as many of the objects as they can remember. Repeat this activity, challenging them to beat their previous record.
- Reverse the game by challenging the class to work out 'Which object have I taken?'
- If appropriate, create a pictograph to show the number of learners with, for example, blue, brown, green eyes.

Success criteria

While completing the activities, assess and record learners who can:

- talk about the similarities and differences between each other's eyes
- recognise and name the main parts of the eye
- explore how senses enable humans to find out about the world around them
- make comparisons between eyes.

 Workbook answers

Page 22 Where are our senses?

1 and **2** Labels and sentences should reflect appropriate matching of senses/body parts:

a smell – nose
b sight – eyes
c touch – skin
d hearing – ears
e taste – tongue

What can you see?

 Learner's Book
pages 38–39

 Workbook
pages 23–24

Objectives

- Explore how senses enable humans and animals to be aware of the world around them. (1Bh4)
- Make comparisons. (1Eo4)
- Suggest ideas and follow instructions. (1Eo2)
- Compare what happened with predictions. (1Eo5)

Background information

The activities on pages 38 and 39 of the Learner's Book help to develop learners' knowledge of the eyes and the sense of sight. The key ideas are the importance of sight, that two eyes work better than just one eye, and what it would be like if they could no longer use their sense of sight.

Focus on the idea that humans (and other animals) rely on the five senses to provide information about the world around us. Learners may know that the sense of sight is important. However, they may not fully appreciate why until they experience the activities on pages 38 and 39.

While some of the activities in this unit separate out the senses, it is important that learners know that the senses work together. While we can function without one or more of the senses, we find out more about the world around us when we can use all of the senses.

Starter activity suggestions

- Ask learners to think about the sense of sight and share ideas about why sight is important.
- Learners could create a collage using pictures from magazines of some of their favourite sights, such as rainbows or animals.
- Ask learners to share with talk partners or in groups what it feels like to be in the dark, such as at home or outdoors at night where there is little or no light. (You can also use this to explain that we need light to see).
- Using magazines or photographs from the internet, learners could create their own montage of different eyes.

Activity notes and answers

Page 38 Activity 1

a Listen to learners talking about what they can see with both eyes open.

b Challenge learners to compare what they saw with both eyes and with only one eye open by asking: *What is the same? What is different? What can you see? Can you see more with both eyes open or with one?*

c Make sure that they are following the instructions (closing the other eye). Ask them to say what is different and what is the same.

d They should conclude that two eyes are better than one. Ask them to say why.

Page 38 Activity 2

a Learners write their name on a piece of paper.

b Check that learners are following instructions and writing their name with their eyes closed.

c Listen to their conclusion.

d Give learners time to explore writing with eyes open, closed, and also with only one eye closed.

When you cannot see

 Activity notes and answers

Page 39 Activity 1

a Make sure that the area the learners are using is safe. Learners blindfold their partner and lead them around the hall or outside.

b Listen to and observe how learners give and receive instructions. Ask them to think about how easy or hard it is to give and receive instructions.

c Ask learners to share how they felt having their sense of sight taken away from them and depending on someone else. For example, ask: *Did you feel safe? Did you trust the other person? Did you feel frightened? Why?*

Page 39 Talk partners Ask learners to share with others what it felt like not being able to see. Link this to learners' understanding that sometimes people need help to see and might need to wear glasses or contact lenses. Some people can see very little and might need the help of a guide dog or a walking stick, use Braille or listen to audio books.

Further activities

- Ask learners to complete Workbook page 23: Our senses, and page 24: Spot the difference!

- Ask a sight-impaired person to talk with the learners and answer their questions.

- Give learners opportunities to explore resources that can enhance their ability to see, such as hand lenses, telescopes and microscopes.

- Develop a list with learners of descriptive words related to sight, such as *colours, colourful, light, dark, shiny, dull* and *bright*.

- Play a 'Describe what you see' game. For example, show learners a flower and ask them to describe it using only the sense of sight. Each learner tries to add a new observation, such as: *It has 10 petals. It is pink. It has green leaves.*

- Play 'On my way to school I saw…' Each child remembers what is already on the list and then adds to it.

- Over the course of a week, give pairs of learners time to use the camera and take interesting photographs to add to a photo album. Learners can then share interesting, beautiful, unusual pictures, or add photos to use for a 'Guess the object' competition.

Success criteria

While completing the activities, assess and record learners who can:

- use their senses to find out about the world around them

- make comparisons between using both eyes and having one or two eyes closed

- follow instructions to carry out activities about the eyes

- compare the results of predictions about what they will see when they close their eyes.

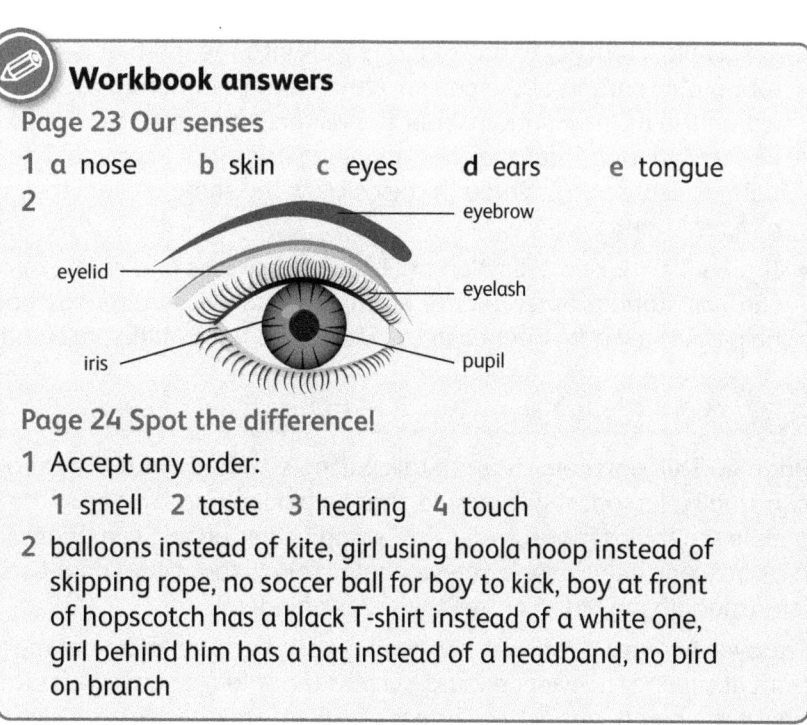

Workbook answers

Page 23 Our senses

1 **a** nose   **b** skin   **c** eyes   **d** ears   **e** tongue

2

eyebrow

eyelid

eyelash

iris

pupil

Page 24 Spot the difference!

1 Accept any order:

   1 smell   2 taste   3 hearing   4 touch

2 balloons instead of kite, girl using hoola hoop instead of skipping rope, no soccer ball for boy to kick, boy at front of hopscotch has a black T-shirt instead of a white one, girl behind him has a hat instead of a headband, no bird on branch

Looking closely

 Learner's Book
pages 40–41

 Workbook
page 25

Objectives

- Explore how senses enable humans and animals to be aware of the world around them. (1Bh4)
- Try to answer questions by collecting evidence through observation. (1Ep1)
- Explore and observe in order to collect evidence (measurements and observations) to answer questions. (1Eo1)
- Record stages in work. (1Eo3)
- Make comparisons. (1Eo4)

Background information

The aim of the activities on pages 40 and 41 of the Learner's Book is to engage learners in making observations using the sense of sight and touch. Observations in science need time, so it is worthwhile to set aside enough time for learners to explore objects. Do not be tempted to hurry the process or tell learners what they can see. Learners observe using their personal experience and interest in the world, and may interpret observations differently from you and other learners.

Begin with providing experiences where learners use their sense of sight to observe. Encourage learners to share observations, comparing what they see. Listening to learners will give you access to what they notice and the sense they make of it. Encourage learners to look multiple times. Where appropriate, remind them to focus on the same thing to encourage them to observe detail, or to focus on something different that they might not yet have noticed. Use scientific words such as *observe* and phrases such as: *Use your observation skills. Look at the detail. What else can you see?*

Providing observational aids such as microscopes, telescopes, binoculars and hand lenses can enhance observations. If used correctly (particularly hand lenses), they offer learners views of objects that cannot normally be seen easily.

Starter activity suggestions

- Ask learners to think and talk about why the sense of sight is important, how it helps in their lives, and how sight helps to keep them safe.
- Ask a fellow teacher to dress up and walk into the room and say hello to the class. It would be useful to take a photograph of the person, either prior to or during the brief visit. When the visitor has left, engage learners in a conversation about the visitor. You might say: *Did you see what they were wearing? What was it? I thought that they had shopping bag – am I correct?* The conversation with learners may help them to realise that although they all saw the same person, they may have noticed and remembered different things.
- If possible, make a collection of observational aids and create a 'carousel' of activities where learners can visit stations to try out, for example, hand lenses, a microscope, binoculars or a telescope. This will help them to know what each can do and how they help observations.

Activity notes and answers

Page 40 Talk partners Listen to talk partners, to find out if they know what each item does. Binoculars are two small telescopes, side by side, that help people see things in the distance. Spectacles (glasses) help people see things more clearly. A telescope helps people see things in space, such as the moon and stars. A microscope helps people see very small things that they cannot see by just using their own eyes. A hand lens (magnifying glass) makes things look bigger.

Page 40 Activity 1 A flower has been chosen because there are many different parts. Learners can move from observing the wider picture, such as the colour and shape of the flower, to more detailed observations about the number of petals, shades of colour, and the parts of the flower.

Answers:

a and **b** Listen to learners describing what they can see using just their eyes. Accept all appropriate answers.

c and **d** Listen to learners comparing what they could see with and without the hand lens. Some learners could make a list of things; others might draw pictures of what they saw with and without a hand lens.

e Check that learners are describing what they can see with a hand lens.

f Check learners' sentences.

The five senses – touch

 Activity notes and answers

Page 41 Activity 1 The aim of this activity is for learners to use their eyes to look at detail of their hands. Support them by asking what they can see, such as skin colour, veins, and so on. Then support them in drawing comparisons between what they can see with only their eyes and with a magnifier. Encourage them to keep alternating between using their eyes and the magnifier to note differences.

Learners use their observational skills to observe the detail of their hands, which links into the next section of the unit on the sense of touch. Learners share what they can see.

Learners compare what they can see with just their eyes and while using a hand lens or microscope (such as a digital microscope).

Page 41 Talk partners Learners share what they can see with their partners. Encourage learners to insist that their partners use scientific vocabulary, such as *sense of sight*, *see*, *observe* and *detail*.

Page 41 Activity 2
Answers:

a Check that learners have drawn the detail of their hands using observations with just their eyes, as well as, for example, with a hand lens or digital microscope.

b Check that learners have labelled the parts of the hand correctly.

Further activities

- Ask learners to complete Workbook page 25: Look closely.
- Leave out interesting objects on an observation table, or create a surprise box with them, for learners to observe using their senses of sight and touch. For example, you can use feathers, fabrics, leaves, sponges, pine cones, seeds and shells. Include colour paddles or coloured cellophane for learners to look through to experience how what they see changes.

Success criteria

While completing the activities, assess and record learners who can:

- use their sense of sight to find out about the world around them
- look carefully to answer questions
- use a hand lens or microscope to look at their hands to answer questions
- draw their hands to show differences
- make comparisons between using their eyes and using a hand lens or microscope to look at things.

 Workbook answers

Page 25 Look closely

1 Check what learners have drawn. Encourage learners to peer assess each other's drawings, checking and commenting on the detail that they have included.

What does it feel like?

 Learner's Book
pages 42–43

 Workbook
page 26

Objectives

- Explore how senses enable humans and animals to be aware of the world around them. (1Bh4)
- Make predictions. (1Ep3)
- Suggest ideas and follow instructions. (1Eo2)
- Record stages in work. (1Eo3)
- Make comparisons. (1Eo4)
- Compare what happened with predictions. (1Eo5)

Background information

The activities on pages 42 and 43 of the Learner's Book develop learners' understanding of the role of the skin in the sense of touch and let them explore textures.

The body's largest organ is the skin. It is what humans use to feel things. Although most people associate touch with hands and fingers, we have sensory receptors on all areas of the skin. This means that we can feel things with our skin, such as textures and how hot or cold things are. A useful word to teach learners is *sensitive*.

The skin has other important roles. It covers and protects everything inside the body and helps to keep our bodies at the right temperature. It stops water and body fluids from leaking out of the body. It stops germs and dirt from getting into the body. It is waterproof. It can sense temperature and when we have been hurt, it lets us feel pain. The skin renews itself all the time, with new skin being created and old skin flaking off. While the skin protects our bodies, the skin also needs protection from germs and cuts. Therefore, washing is important, as well as covering up cuts and grazes with plasters and bandages to keep out dirt and infection.

Starter activity suggestions

- Take learners outdoors to make a tactile journey stick. They use a twig, or a stick from indoors. They tape on or tie string onto the stick and the object, collecting different textures. For example, learners might add leaves, twigs, stones, grass and moss to their journey stick. Back indoors, they could add labels to describe the texture of each object.

- Give learners a very simple jigsaw puzzle with only four to six pieces. Ask them to complete the jigsaw puzzle using touch only, while keeping their eyes closed. They could work with a partner, with the partner giving directions.

- Ask learners to find out if their skin is the same all over their body, giving reasons why or why not. They should be able to say it is thicker on the soles of the feet (to protect the feet when we walk), and loose over joints such as the elbow (so that they can move easily).

- Take the class on a texture hunt around the school grounds. Give learners a list of words or set of cards for which they have to find an object with a matching texture.

Activity notes and answers

Page 42 Activity 1
Answers:

a and b Check that learners have chosen five materials with different textures, and that they have named each texture appropriately.

c Check that the learners match the correct texture word to the material that they have used. Support them by providing key language for learners to use.

Page 42 Challenge yourself! Challenge learners to predict whether or not the elbow will be as good as the hand at feeling textures. They must then compare the prediction with what they felt with their elbows. Encourage them to think of possible reasons for what they observed. They should be able to work out that we use our hands for touching objects more frequently than our elbows, so our hands are more sensitive to feeling textures.

What are you touching?

 Activity notes and answers

Page 43 Activity 1

a Support learners when collecting the six objects, so that they choose different textures rather than objects with the same texture.

b If some learners do not want to be blindfolded by their partner, suggest that they close their eyes instead.

c Stress the need to take turns. One partner should talk to the other partner and describe what they feel, while the other partner listens.

d Remind learners that when their partners say what each object is, they should complete the table of results (see Activity 2, below).

Page 43 Activity 2

a Some learners might require support when taking the other role. You could ask their partner to explain what to do.

b Listen to learners comparing their results. Did they get them all correct? Which ones did they not get right, and why? Were there any that they both got wrong?

c Ask learners to look at which objects they did not guess correctly, and to talk about why they think these were harder to guess than the others.

Further activities

- Ask learners to complete Workbook page 26: Hand sizes.

- Create sensory bags. These could be objects with different textures that learners feel and describe to a partner. Alternatively, they could be sealed plastic bags with a range of materials that they can see, such as a slimy mixture, washing-up liquid, very soft dough, and sequins in water.

- Make matching pairs of opaque plastic gloves filled with substances such as couscous, pasta, rice, cotton wool, and dry breakfast cereal (such as oats). Learners feel each sealed glove and find its matching pair.

Success criteria

While completing the activities, assess and record learners who can:

- explore using their sense of touch to find out about objects in the classroom

- make predictions about what they can feel when blindfolded

- follow instructions on how to play the blindfold game.

- record different textures on their texture hand and use the correct words

- compare the textures of different objects using touch

- compare what they felt with their predictions.

 Workbook answers

Page 26 Hand sizes

1 b and c Check whether their idea is appropriate. They might choose to draw around their hand on the squares and then count the squares.

2 a and b Check learners' answers.

The five senses – smell

Learner's Book
pages 44–45

Workbook
page 27

Objectives

- Explore how senses enable humans and animals to be aware of the world around them. (1Bh4)
- Make predictions. (1Ep3)
- Suggest ideas and follow instructions. (1Eo2)
- Record stages in work. (1Eo3)
- Make comparisons. (1Eo4)
- Compare what happened with predictions. (1Eo5)

Background information

The activities on pages 44 and 45 of the Learner's Book develop learners' knowledge about the nose and the sense of smell, which is made possible because the nose and brain work together. When we breathe in, tiny particles enter the nose. At the back of the nose are tiny hairs which send messages to the brain. The brain works out what the smell is. The nose is also important because it is one way that humans take air in and out of the lungs.

Our sense of smell is one way that humans and other animals find out about their world. It includes sensing danger, such as smoke. One of the important ideas about the five senses is that they do not work in isolation. For example, seeing something can affect what you think it smells like, and the sense of taste is affected by the sense of smell. A simple but effective way to show this is to hold your nose when you eat. Not being able to smell what you are eating can dull or reduce our sense of taste.

Starter activity suggestions

- Elicit learners' ideas about the sense of smell. Collect their ideas in a display with a huge nose in the centre. Each time learners find out something about the sense of smell, they can add to the display. Perhaps let them use different colours to show learning before, during and at the end of this set of work.
- Show learners a video clip of the star-nosed mole from the internet. Ask questions such as: *Where does it live? Why does it only have small eyes? Which senses do you think it uses the most?*
- If possible, burn a different scented candle each lesson. Ask learners to vote for their favourite.
- Ask learners if all things have a smell, if some smell stronger than others. They could draw or paint their ideas and then find out using their sense of smell.

Activity notes and answers

Page 44 Activity 1
Answers:

a panda   b horse   c human   d rabbit   e elephant   f giraffe

What can you smell?

Activity notes and answers

Page 45 Activity 1 Learners smell each pot. Some learners might need to see the objects near the pots to try matching the smell. Check their tables in relation to whatever 'smelly' objects have been put inside the pots.

Page 45 Activity 2 Learners repeat the previous activity, but this time make their own smell pots and carry out the activity independently.

They make their own smell pots from things provided by you, such as herbs, spices, flowers, coffee, juice and vinegar. They can put in small amounts of the materials using a teaspoon or pipette.

Learners test their partner to see if they recognise the smells in each pot. Their partner says what is inside each smell pot. They complete a table to show which smells their partner recognised.

Be careful !

Make sure that the substances you provide for making the smell pots will not be harmful.

Further activities

- Ask learners to complete Workbook page 27: All kinds of smells.

- Tell learners that they are going to make a new perfume by mixing things that smell. They should then ask others to smell it, saying what it smells of and whether they like it. Ask learners to think of a way that they could record how they made their perfume and also what others said about it.

- Let learners make a smell story, such as a story related to a walk outdoors. Ask learners to stick the things that smell onto a piece of card, or on a card wristband with double-sided tape on it. Learners could stick on grass, a flower, strong-smelling leaves (such as pine needles) and some mud.

- Ask learners to plant smelly plants, including herbs such as rosemary, sage, thyme and marjoram, as well as scented flowers local to your country, to create a sensory garden. Talk about the importance of sensory gardens for people who have sight impairments.

- Have a baking session with learners. Focus on how, during the making and baking process, different ingredients give off different smells and how these smells change when adding ingredients together, and during heating or cooling.

Assessment ideas

To assess that learners know different smells and can name things that make smells, ask them to make up a short story to tell each other about something they smelled. For example, *I walked into the kitchen and the smell hit me. I knew that something was burning, and there it was, my toast for breakfast, all black and burnt.* They could share their stories with the class.

Workbook answers

Page 27 All kinds of smells

1 a and b Encourage learners to talk about which smells they like and do not like before drawing them in the table.

Success criteria

While completing the activities, assess and record learners who can:

- use the sense of smell to find out about the world around them
- make predictions about what makes the smell in each pot
- follow instructions
- record what they found using a table
- make comparisons between different smells
- compare their predictions with what was in the scent pots.

Funny smells!

 Learner's Book
pages 46–47

 Workbook
page 28

Objectives

- Explore how senses enable humans and animals to be aware of the world around them. (1Bh4)
- Decide what to do to try to answer a science question. (1Ep4)
- Suggest ideas and follow instructions. (1Eo2)
- Record stages in work. (1Eo3)
- Make comparisons. (1Eo4)
- Compare what happened with predictions. (1Eo5)

Background information

The activities on page 46 of the Learner's Book consolidate experiences involving using the sense of smell. They also provide an opportunity for learners to set up their own simple activity by making smell pots to test on someone else. This allows learners to develop elements of scientific enquiry skills by using their own ideas while modelling and adapting a senses activity that they have previously experienced.

The activities on page 47 of the Learner's Book introduce learners to the sense of taste. Taste is one of the five senses. Humans taste things through the taste buds on the top of their tongue. There are five basic tastes: sweet, sour, salty, bitter and umami (savoury/taste of meat or fish, which is not covered in the unit as it is a more difficult taste for learners to recognise). In this unit we focus on the tastes of sweet, sour and salty.

Some learners might have had a wide range of experiences of different tastes through food cooked at home. Other learners' experiences may have been more limited. They may require experience of tasting a wide range of food and drinks. They may also need to be taught the words to go with the basic tastes, as well as other words relating to textures, such as *chewy*, *hard* and *soft*.

Starter activity suggestions

- Ask learners to discuss what they know about the sense of taste and the tongue. Collect their ideas and display them, then return to these ideas during the unit.
- Learners could make a page in their books about the sense of taste, which might look something like this picture.

Activity notes and answers

Page 46 Activity 1 Check that learners have identified the correct fruit in their table. The pots could include fruit such as banana, orange, lime, lemon and apple, as well as other strong-smelling fruits.

Page 46 Activity 2 Learners make their own horrible smell pot, using materials which they could mix. For example, vinegar, onions and other strong-smelling materials, such as some spices and herbs, might have an unpleasant smell when mixed together. Ask partners to comment on the 'horrible' smell pot. Could they recognise any of the smells, and how horrible was the smell?

Be careful !

Make sure that the substances you provide for making the smell pots will not be harmful.

The five senses – taste

 Activity notes and answers

Elicit what learners already know about taste prior to beginning the activities in the Learner's Book to assess their knowledge. Their ideas could be placed on a huge face with tongue sticking out as part of a classroom display. Make sure that learners use the correct scientific words, such as *senses, sense of taste, taste buds, tongue*, as well as the names of the three basic tastes.

Page 47 Activity 1

a Learners taste each piece of food. You could give them lemons, limes, a sweet, oranges, grapes, potato chips, and so on. At first, give learners foods that fit easily into the categories. You could then repeat the activity and offer more subtle tastes that are harder to group, or a surprise taste, such as sour apples.

b Listen to talk partner's discussing different foods. Check that they understand and use the correct words for different tastes.

c Check the table that they have completed.

Page 47 Challenge yourself! You could give learners a card or page with the words on and ask them to talk about the tastes when they eat at home. They could draw a food under each taste to bring back and share with the class.

Further activities

- Ask learners to complete Workbook page 28: Nice smells.

- Read the boy's question on Learner's Book page 47 together with the class. Ask learners to vote for their favourite taste. Collect the data and produce a class graph. Use the graph to ask data handling questions.

- Learners could keep a diary of sweet, sour and salty tastes that they have eaten during the week.

Success criteria

While completing the activities, assess and record learners who can:

- use their senses of smell and taste to find out about world around them

- decide how to answer a science question (*How can you make your own smell pot?*)

- suggest ideas about making their own smell pots and follow instructions

- record what they have done using a table

- make comparisons between different smells and tastes

- compare what they thought a taste or smell would be with real observations of tastes or smells.

 Workbook answers

Page 28 Nice smells

1 a 8
  b lemons
  c 6
  d roses
2 Check learners' drawings.

What does it taste like?

 Learner's Book
pages 48–50

 Workbook
pages 29–30

 Digital Resource

Objectives

- Explore how senses enable humans and animals to be aware of the world around them. (1Bh4)
- Decide what to do to try to answer a science question. (1Ep4)
- Suggest ideas and follow instructions. (1Eo2)
- Record stages in work. (1Eo3)
- Make comparisons. (1Eo4)
- Model and communicate ideas in order to share, explain and develop them. (1Eo6)

Background information

The activities on page 48 of the Learner's Book illustrate to learners that the sense of taste and smell work together, allowing us to taste the flavours of food. The tongue and brain detect taste, but without the nose and sense of smell, we would not be able to taste most things that we eat. Even though the senses of taste and smell are separate, they work together so that we can taste food. As we breathe in the smell of the food, the nose and tongue work together to send signals to the brain which works out what you are tasting. Most people who have a cold complain that they cannot taste the flavours of their food. This is because their noses are blocked from the cold, and they are unable to breathe in the smells properly.

The activities on page 49 give learners opportunities to explore the sense of hearing. The key ideas that learners need to master are that hearing is one of the five senses, that we hear with our ears, and that this helps humans (and other animals) to find out about the world around them. Knowledge on sound and vibration is developed in later stages of the Cambridge Primary Science curriculum. Explain to learners that they must take care of their ears and never make loud sounds next to someone's ears, or put anything unsafe into their own ears.

Starter activity suggestions

- Recap what learners know about the senses so far. Add these ideas to any displays related to the senses, where learners' ideas are on show.
- Ask learners to think about any other questions they would like to answer about taste. Give them time to find ways to answer their questions, and share their answers with the rest of the class.
- Ask learners to think about how the senses work together. Ask them to think about which senses work with the sense of hearing, and to describe how.
- Show learners videos of working animals who support people who are, for example, hearing or sight impaired.
- Show learners a video clip of rescue dogs using their sense of smell to find humans in disaster areas, such as after an earthquake.

Activity notes and answers

Page 48 Activity 1
Answer:
Learners should conclude from carrying out the instructions that when they hold their nose, the sweet does not taste very strong. When they can use their sense of smell, the taste of the sweet is stronger.

The five senses – hearing

 Activity notes and answers

Page 49 Activity 1 Learners follow instructions and record their results in the table. To support learners, you could provide a selection of sound makers for them to use. Alternatively, you could let them collect their own sound makers before starting the activity.

Page 49 Activity 2 Learners shake each box. They listen and then match the containers that have the same sound. Some sound boxes are commercially available, but they are easily made using small containers (such as film canisters) or tissue boxes with card taped across the opening.

What have you learnt about 'ourselves'?

 Activity notes and answers

Page 50 Activity 1
Learners could add a sentence to go with their pictures, for example:
a My favourite *smell* is cookies.   b My favourite *taste* is noodles.
c My favourite sound or thing to *hear* is music.
d My favourite thing to *see* is a big smile.   e My favourite thing to *touch* is a soft cushion.
Page 50 Activity 2
Answers:

a head	b shoulder	c arm	d wrist	e leg	f ankle
g hand	h elbow	i chest	j knee	k foot	

Further activities

- Ask learners to complete Workbook page 29: Questions about taste and page 30: More about senses.
- Show learners the Unit 2 digital resource video clip: Mole. Draw attention to how the mole is using its sense of smell.

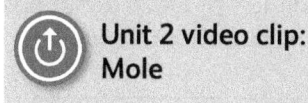 **Unit 2 video clip: Mole**

Success criteria

While completing the activities, assess and record learners who can:
- explore using the senses of taste, smell and sound
- decide what to do to try to answer the science challenge question
- suggest ideas and follow instructions
- record what they have found out in a table
- compare what happened with what they predicted
- model and communicate the ideas of taste and smell working together to another learner.

 Workbook answers
Page 29 Questions about taste
1 Check learners' questions.
Page 30 More about senses
1 a five
   b smell and touch
   c see   d nose
   e taste buds   f salty
2 Accept learners' answers.

Assessment ideas

Ask learners to self-assess using the 'What can you remember?' checklist on page 50 of the Learner's Book, as well as the self-assessment table on page 30 of the Workbook.

Unit 3 Living and growing

Objectives overview

Learning objective	Objective code	Learner's Book pages	Teacher's Pack pages	Workbook pages	Digital Resource Pack
Biology: Plants					
Know that plants are living things.	1Bp1	51, 52	66, 67	33	
Know that there are living things and things that have never been alive.	1Bp2	51, 52	66, 67	32, 33	Unit 3 slide 3
Explore ways that different animals and plants inhabit local environments.	1Bp3	53, 54, 55, 57	68, 69, 70, 71, 72, 73	34, 35, 36	Unit 3 slide 4, video clips 1, 2
Biology: Humans and animals					
Know about the need for a healthy diet, including the right types of food and water.	1Bh3	62, 63, 64, 65, 66, 67, 68, 69, 70, 71	77, 78, 79, 80, 81, 82, 83, 84, 85, 86, 87	38, 39, 40, 41, 42	Unit 3 slide 7, PCM2
Know that humans and animals produce offspring which grow into adults.	1Bh5	56, 57, 58, 59, 60, 61	70, 71, 72, 73, 74, 75, 76, 77, 78	35, 36, 37	Unit 3 slides 5, 6, PCM1, video clip 2
Scientific enquiry: Ideas and evidence					
Try to answer questions by collecting evidence through observation.	1Ep1	51, 52, 53, 59, 60, 61, 69, 70	66, 67, 68, 69, 74, 75, 77, 78, 85, 86, 87	33, 34	Unit 3 slides 5, 6
Scientific enquiry: Plan investigative work					
Decide what to do to try to answer a science question.	1Ep4			42	
Scientific enquiry: Obtain and present evidence					
Explore and observe in order to collect evidence (measurements and observations) to answer questions.	1Eo1	67, 69	85, 86, 87	36, 38, 39, 40	PCM1
Suggest ideas and follow instructions.	1Eo2			42	
Record stages in work.	1Eo3	51, 52, 54, 58, 67, 68, 70	66, 67, 68, 69, 72, 73, 83, 84 ,85, 86, 87		

Learning objective	Objective code	Learner's Book pages	Teacher's Pack pages	Workbook pages	Digital Resource Pack
Scientific enquiry: Consider evidence and approach					
Make comparisons.	1Eo4	51, 52, 53, 55, 56, 57, 60, 61, 65, 66, 70	66, 67, 68, 69, 70, 71, 72, 73, 74, 75, 76, 77, 78, 81, 82, 85, 86, 87	34, 35, 37, 38, 40	Unit 3 slides 3, 5
Model and communicate ideas in order to share, explain and develop them.	1Eo6	52, 58, 63, 64, 65	66, 67, 72, 73, 79, 80, 81, 82	36, 39	Unit 3 slides 3, 7

Living things

Learner's Book
pages 51–52

Workbook
pages 32–33

Digital Resource

Objectives

- Know that plants are living things. (1Bp1)
- Know that there are living things and things that have never been alive. (1Bp2)
- Try to answer questions by collecting evidence through observation. (1Ep1)
- Record stages in work. (1Eo3)
- Make comparisons. (1Eo4)
- Model and communicate ideas in order to share, explain and develop them. (1Eo6)

Background information

The aims of the activities on pages 51 and 52 of the Learner's Book are to develop learners' understanding of the idea that some things are alive, and that these are called living things – for example, humans and other animals.

For learners, the first step is for them to recognise that some things are living because they do certain things, called life processes. These include movement, breathing (needing air), being sensitive to their surroundings (reacting), feeding, growing, having young (babies) and excreting (producing waste). Across the primary years, learners will develop their knowledge of all the life processes. Learners have already been introduced to moving, eating, breathing, growing and using senses. In this unit, having young (babies) will be introduced as well, with excretion added in later stages. In Stage 1, it is easier for learners to relate these life processes to themselves before applying them to other animals. Use the term *life processes*, explaining that these are things that living things do. This will help learners in later stages. Make sure that learners are regularly reminded that plants are also living things.

Starter activity suggestions

- Display the Unit 3 digital resource slideshow, slide 3: Are you alive? Use it as a starting point for discussions about how learners know that they are alive.

 Unit 3 slideshow, slide 3: Are you alive?

Answers to slide 3:
a For example, learners could suggest that they move, breathe, talk, eat and use their senses.
b Provide learners with key words to copy from, either on the board or as a simple word mat for their tables.

- Use the language of life processes, such as *living things, alive, move, eat, breathe, grow* and *using senses*.
- Show learners some objects, such as a stone, mug or bottle of water. Ask them to discuss with their partner whether these objects are alive or not, and how they know.
- Show learners a toy doll. Ask whether it is alive or not, and how they know.
- Ask learners what do they think would happen if, for example, they did not do one or more of the life processes themselves, such as move, grow, eat, breathe and use their senses to find out about the world around them.

Activity notes and answers

Page 51 Talk partners Listen to learners discussing how they know they are alive. Make notes of any ideas that might need to be challenged and developed through further conversation and activity. Check and unpick what learners say by asking them questions such as: *Why do you think that? What makes you say that?*

Page 51 Activity 1

a Support learners by asking them to think about what else moves, eats, uses their senses and breathes. Make silly suggestions, such as a brick or table, which can help learners to make appropriate suggestions.

b and **c** Check what learners have drawn as being alive. If necessary, engage in conversations about their drawings to elicit their thinking.

Page 51 Challenge yourself! Encourage learners to record what they find and bring these things to school, such as lists, photographs and drawings to share with other class members.

Alive or never been alive?

 Activity notes and answers

Page 52 Activity 1 Working with partners, listen to what learners pick out as 'living' and 'never been alive' as they search the school grounds. If learners are not including plants, discuss the idea that plants are alive. Listen to learners' reasons for choosing things that have never been alive. Give learners the opportunity to take photographs and make video clips to record what they find.

Page 52 Activity 2 Ask learners to think about whether the suggestions the other pair made are correct. Ask: *Did you have an interesting idea?* Encourage them to ask the other pair to say how they know those things are alive.

Further activities

- Ask learners to complete Workbook page 32: A living thing, and page 33: Alive and never alive.
- With the learners, create a big book about living and growing, starting with pictures of living things and listing life processes.
- In the big book, include a photograph of the whole class. Write comments about how they know class members are alive.
- Ask learners to add to a table top display of things that have never been alive. They could add items from around the classroom, outdoors and from home.
- Leave out, as part of a table top display, pictures of things that are living and things that have never been alive for learners to sort into sets.

Success criteria

While completing the activities, assess and record learners who can:

- tell someone that plants are living things
- sort living things and things that have never been alive into groups
- make observations and use them to say why some things are alive and others have never been alive
- take photographs or make a list of things that are alive or have never been alive
- make comparisons between things that are alive or not alive
- tell others about why something is alive or has never been alive.

 Workbook answers

Page 32 A living thing

1 **a** Answers such as it moves, eats, breathes, uses its senses and grows.

2 **a** moves
  b eats
  c breathe
  d grown

Page 33 Alive and never alive

1 **a** rock – never alive　　**b** tree – alive
  c cola – never alive　　**d** fish – alive
  e plant – alive　　　　**f** child – alive
  g kettle – never alive　**h** scooter – never alive

2 and 3 Check learners' drawings.

Places to live

 Learner's Book
pages 53–54

 Workbook
page 34

 Digital Resource

Objectives

- Explore ways that different animals and plants inhabit local environments. (1Bp3)
- Try to answer questions by collecting evidence through observation. (1Ep1)
- Record stages in work. (1Eo3)
- Make comparisons. (1Eo4)

Background information

The activities on pages 53 and 54 of the Learner's Book develop learners' knowledge of what a habitat is and about different kinds of habitats. A habitat is a home where plants and animals live. A useful place to start discussions is by asking learners to think about their own habitats (their homes) and what each home has.

Examples of habitats include deserts, woodlands, forests, grasslands, the seashore and oceans. Small localised habitats are called micro-habitats, such as under a stone or a pile of logs, or in ponds, hedgerows and even individual trees.

Starter activity suggestions

- Learners could draw their own home – their habitat. Ask them to tell their talk partner why their home is a good habitat.
- Display the Unit 3 digital resource slideshow, slide 4: Habitats. Use it to show and discuss different kinds of habitats and what might live there.

 Unit 3 slideshow, slide 4: Habitats

Answers to slide 4:
a Learners might suggest the following:
  - log – beetles, worms, spiders, woodlice, snakes
  - pond – frogs, ducks, crocodiles, dragonfly
  - tree – birds, some large cats (such as a leopard)
b Learners might suggest: river, sea, desert, garden, bush, rainforest.
c These answers will depend on what habitats they have suggested. Encourage learners, as a class or in small groups, to make suggestions to help each other, thereby sharing knowledge and ideas.

- Show learners the Unit 3 digital resource video clip 1: Caterpillar. Discuss why the caterpillar might have a plant as a habitat. *What is it doing to the leaf?*

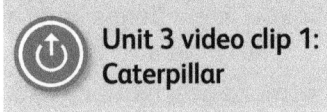 **Unit 3 video clip 1: Caterpillar**

- Take learners into the school grounds to search for different habitats, such as under stones or logs, or in a hedgerow, tree or pond. Ask: *What evidence or signs can you find of things living there, both animals and plants? Why do they live there? Does it offer shelter, food and water?*
- Give learners pictures of a habitat. (These could be photographs from your local environment.) Ask them to talk about which animals and plants live in the habitat, and what the habitat has for things to live there.
- Show learners a picture of a pond. Discuss what they know about ponds and what lives there, such as birds, fish, insects and plants. Ask learners to talk about shelter, food and water (relating these things to the life processes as well).

Activity notes and answers

Page 53 Talk partners Listen to talk partners to find out if they understand the idea of animals living near them, and if they can name any. Use this as a formative assessment point to inform next steps.

Page 53 Activity 1 If your local environment does not have trees, water (such as a pond, stream or river), and so on, replace the suggested habitats with those from your local environment. Learners might find it easier if they have visited the habitats prior to this drawing activity.

Ducks

 Activity notes and answers

Page 54 Activity 1 Learners make a duck habitat, so make sure that there are videos, books and pictures that they can refer to. Show learners the Unit 3 digital resource video clip 2: Ducks, drawing attention to the habitat. Also ensure a range of natural materials for learners to use, as well as shallow containers that they can use as their pond, stream or river. Ask learners to write a sentence to go alongside their habitat. The sentence should describe what lives there and why.

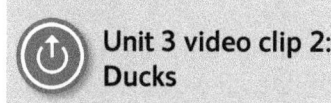 **Unit 3 video clip 2: Ducks**

Page 54 Talk partners

a Partners should explain to each other what the habitat is like, for example by referring to water, reeds, plants, pond or river bank.

b Partners should explain that the habitat provides shelter, such as reeds, grass, water for food and drink, and air for ducks to breathe.

Further activities

- Ask learners to complete Workbook page 34: Animal homes.

- Ask learners to choose a native animal to find information about. This could include using pictures in books. They could be given a selection of animals to choose from, such as a badger, fox, deer, hedgehog, sand lizard, bumblebee, seahorse or snail. Alternatively, they could be allowed to research any native animal of their choice. Encourage them to use school library books or the internet. They could then share their findings with each other through discussion or a presentation.

Success criteria

While completing the activities, assess and record learners who can:

- describe the habitats that different animals live in
- find out about different animals
- make a model of a habitat
- compare what different habitats look like.

 Workbook answers

Page 34 Animal homes

1 bird – tree

   camel – desert

   rabbit – burrow

   wasp – wasp nest

   beetle – woodpile

   fish – pond

Who lives in this habitat?

Learner's Book
pages 55–56

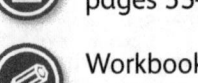

Workbook
page 35

Digital Resource

Objectives

- Explore ways that different animals and plants inhabit local environments. (1Bp3)
- Know that humans and animals produce offspring which grow into adults. (1Bh5)
- Make comparisons. (1Eo4)

Background information

The activities on page 55 of the Learner's Book develop learners' knowledge of different animals and their habitats. It would be useful to add examples of habitats and animals from your local environment and country in general. If your school grounds have micro-habitats such as stones, soil or trees, take learners outside to search for animals. Discuss with learners what kind of things the habitat offers animals living there, such as shelter, food, air, water and somewhere to raise their young. Consider places you can visit locally outside the school grounds to further develop learners' knowledge of animals and their habitats.

The activities on page 56 of the Learner's Book develop learners' knowledge of adults and their offspring. The key focal points of the activities should be key vocabulary such as *adult, babies, young* and *offspring*. Make sure that learners know that animal babies grow to look like their parents.

Starter activity suggestions

- Take learners into the local environment to look for animals, or evidence of animals, and their habitats. Ask questions, such as: *What kind of habitats can you find? What lives there? Why do the animals live in that habitat?*
- Use the Unit 3 digital resource slideshow, slide 5: Animal offspring. Ask learners to name the animal young (elephant calf, seal pup, polar bear cub, banded kingfisher chick). Engage learners in discussion about physical similarities and differences between the adult and offspring. You could also challenge learners by asking what they think the offspring can and cannot do that its parent can.

 Unit 3 slideshow, slide 5: Animal offspring

Answers to slide 5:
a For example:
  polar bear – furry, white, big, big paws, small ears, black nose and eyes
  seal – flippers, whiskers, tail
  duck – beaks, neck, body shape, swimming.
  horse – four legs, mane, tail, ears, hooves.
b For example:
  polar bear – size
  seal – adult has smooth skin /fur, baby has fluffy skin/fur, big eyes, different nose
  duck – feathers not formed properly on ducklings, soft and fluffy.
  horse – size

- Ask learners to share ideas about what parent animals need to do for their young, such as a lioness finding food for cubs until they can fend for themselves.
- Ask learners what their parents do for them. Compare this with different animals.

Activity notes and answers

Page 55 Activity 1
Answers: **a** soil – worm   **b** river – fish   **c** woodpile – beetle   **d** cave – bear

Page 55 Talk partners Support discussion by asking learners to think about the things that animals need to stay alive, such as shelter, water, air, food and somewhere to raise their young. Listen to learners' discussions to assess the level of what they know.

Offspring

 Activity notes and answers

Page 56 Activity 1
Answers:

a and **b** deer – fawn   spider – spiderlings   seal – pup

Page 56 Challenge yourself! Help learners to use pictures as well as text to find information, or to use a video clip or poster for research. Talk with learners about how they could record what they find out.

 ICT links

Ask learners to search on the internet to find pictures of animals and their offspring. They could print these out to make their own mini-booklets. They could also watch video clips to find out information about animals and their young. Encourage some learners to make a short video clip of themselves talking about an animal, perhaps using a toy animal as a prop.

Further activities

- Ask learners to complete Workbook page 35: Offspring.
- Learners could make model animals and their habitats.
- Cut out pictures of adult animals and pictures of offspring, so that the learners can match adult to offspring.
- Cut out pictures of offspring so that the learners can match the offspring to its name, such as *cub*, *foal* or *chick*.
- Ask learners to choose an animal from the Learner's Book and find out more about the animal. They could draw a picture and write sentences (or you could write sentences for them to copy).

Assessment ideas

Ask learners to make a dough adult animal with its offspring, and place it in a habitat which could be made from dough or other materials. For example, they might choose to make a local bird, chick and nest. If they have a cat at home, they could make the adult, kitten and bed. (Although this is a domestic animal, learners can think of this as the habitat.) They could show and talk about their work to others in the class. Challenge learners to use appropriate vocabulary, such as *adult*, *offspring* and *habitat*.

Success criteria

While completing the activities, assess and record learners who can:
- recognise animal habitats and say why things live there
- talk about different animals and name their young
- compare different animals and match adult animals to their offspring.

 Workbook answers

Page 35 Offspring
1 food air shelter water
2 duck – duckling
  cat – kitten
  lion – cub
  seal – pup

The life cycle of a frog

Learner's Book
pages 57–58

Workbook
page 36

Objectives

- Explore ways that different animals and plants inhabit local environments. (1Bp3)
- Know that humans and animals produce offspring which grow into adults. (1Bh5)
- Record stages in work. (1Eo3)
- Make comparisons. (1Eo4)
- Model and communicate ideas in order to share them and explain and develop them. (1Eo6)

Background information

The activities on pages 57 and 58 of the Learner's Book develop learners' understanding of a common life cycle where the young do not look like the adult when they are born, but change and eventually look like the parent. Frogs lay their eggs in water or wet places. The clump of eggs is called frogspawn. Several thousand eggs can be laid at a time in a jelly-like substance, in large clumps . They are vulnerable to predation, but with so many, there is a chance that some will survive. The eggs develop into tadpoles that undergo a change (metamorphosis) into a frog. Only a few develop into adults because predators such as insects (such as dragonflies and water beetles), fish and ducks will eat the eggs and tadpoles.

Support learners in understanding that some animals do not look like their parents when they are born, but change to look like the adults as they grow. Frogs, toads, butterflies and moths all undergo this kind of change, as do many other animals. Help learners to develop their knowledge of animals that undergo metamorphosis in their local environment or country, in addition to the examples in the Learner's Book. Use the vocabulary of *life cycle, change, adult, young* and *offspring* regularly with learners, so that they become confident in using the words themselves.

Starter activity suggestions

- Show learners video clips of the life cycle of a frog from the internet. Stop the clip at appropriate points and discuss different aspects by asking questions such as: *Are all frogs the same? Where do they live? What is their habitat like? How do they change?*
- Give learners pictures of a frog's life cycle that they have to put into order. Ask them to discuss the various stages with talk partners.

 ## Activity notes and answers

Page 57 Activity 1
Answer:
a tadpole

Page 57 Talk partners
Example answers:
a water
b frogspawn; black dots in jelly
c black, round head and long tail (a bit like a fish)
d It grows back legs, then front legs and loses its tail.
e no

Make a frog life cycle

 Activity notes and answers

Page 58 Activity 1

a Learners can choose how they will communicate the life cycle. Discuss the examples on the page and ask learners to suggest other approaches.

b Give learners time to plan what they want to do.

c Ask learners to make a list of what they need, or to collect what they will use. Make sure that everything is available (from the resources you have put out), such as paper, crayons, pencils, paper plates and dough.

d Discuss with learners what a circle shape is. Remind them why it is called a *life cycle*, so that they use this idea in their work.

Page 58 Talk partners Listen to learners discussing with their partners what they think is good about their work. Make suggestions for improving, such as one star (something good) and a wish (something they could improve on).

Further activities

- Ask learners to complete Workbook page 36: The life cycle of a butterfly.
- Ask learners to use modelling dough to make the life cycle of a frog or another animal, such as a butterfly.
- Ask learners to work in small groups and role-play the life cycle of a frog, with different learners taking different parts.
- Ask learners to research local frogs at home and share this information back in the class.
- Ask learners to make a shoebox diorama (3D model) showing frogs in their habitat.

ICT links

Ask learners to use the internet to find pictures of different kinds of frogs or frog habitats. Pairs of learners could watch a video clip about the life cycle of a frog to inform their diorama and dough models.

Success criteria

While completing the activities, assess and record learners who can:

- say where a frog lives and describe what its habitat is like
- say that a frog has young and describe how they change to grow into an adult frog
- make a life cycle using, for example, dough and paper plates
- compare the different stages of a life cycle and talk about similarities and differences
- make a model of the life cycle of a frog to show and explain to others.

 Workbook answers

Page 36 The life cycle of a butterfly

1

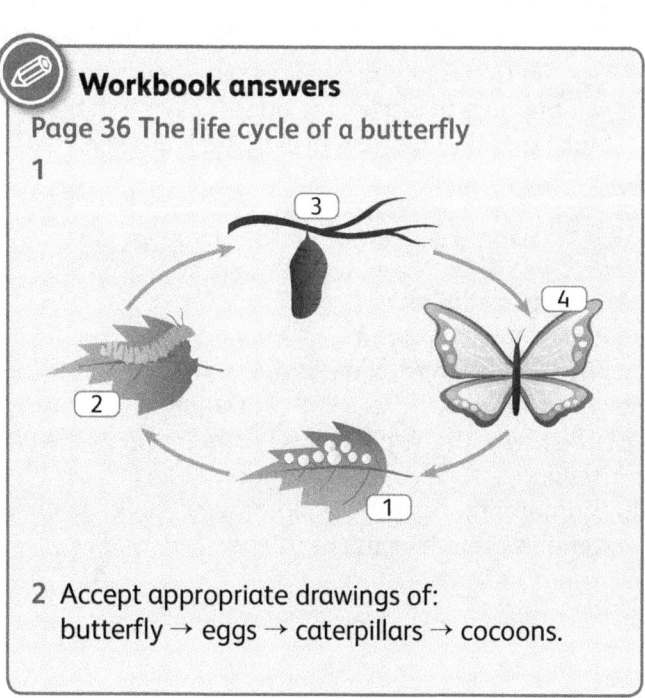

2 Accept appropriate drawings of:
butterfly → eggs → caterpillars → cocoons.

What am I?

 Learner's Book
pages 59–60

 Workbook
page 37

 Digital Resource

Objectives

- Know that humans and animals produce offspring which grow into adults. (1Bh5)
- Try to answer questions by collecting evidence through observation. (1Ep1)
- Make comparisons. (1Eo4)

Background information

The activities on page 59 of the Learner's Book consolidate and apply learners' knowledge about animals and their offspring. This is done through the use of 'What am I?' riddles.

Learners will enjoy creating their own riddles, but will need to be shown and talked through some examples. Create some as a whole class to start. You could put out a big scrapbook in which learners could write their own riddles. They could also create some with parents at home to bring in to share with the class.

The activities on page 60 of the Learner's Book develop learners' understanding that humans have offspring (babies). Like other living things, learners began as babies and go through the same stages as other animals, to eventually become adults.

Starter activity suggestions

- Prior to beginning this section, ask learners to bring in photographs of themselves as a baby, toddler and as they are now. They can also bring in photographs of their family (grandparents, aunts, uncles, cousins, brothers, sisters and parents). The aim is not to show how they look like other members of their family, because not all children do. However, the photographs will help to show the different stages in the life of a human, from child to adult. If learners are unable to bring in photographs, bring in some of your own to show them.

- Create a 'Guess the baby' picture gallery. Learners put a photo of themselves as a baby on the gallery wall. Others in the class try to guess which photograph belongs to which of their classmates.

- Put out pictures of human life cycles for learners to put into the correct order.

- Use the Unit 3 digital resource slideshow, slide 6: Growing up. Discuss the different photographs. Ask the class to discuss the questions and share responses. They can do it with talk partners or in groups. Make sure that learners explain their answers.

 Unit 3 slideshow, slide 6: Growing up

Answers to slide 6:
Learners might suggest:
a The baby with the woman is the youngest. It is the smallest and has to be held safely.
b The woman with grey hair and wrinkles.
c The boy with the phone and earphones. He is bigger than the children. He is wearing clothes like a teenager, such as a hooded jacket.
d Grandmother/great-grandmother, depending on learners' own experience. Many might say great-grandmother because of the age, hair and wrinkles.

Activity notes and answers

Page 59 Activity 1
Answers:
a sheep
b Responses will depend on individual learners.

Page 59 Activity 2
a Give support to individuals, where necessary, as they make up their riddle.
b Give learners time to share their riddles with other members of the class.
c Work with learners who have difficulty making sense of a riddle.

Page 59 Challenge yourself! You could give learners a picture of a young animal for them to take home to make up a riddle. They could also find pictures of their own and make up other riddles. They can then bring these to class to share with others in the class.

Babies and toddlers

 Activity notes and answers

Page 60 Talk partners Listen to pairs discussing what they were like as a baby and how they have changed. They can use the photographs that they brought to school to support discussions. Encourage learners to use words such as *baby*, *toddler*, *teenager*, *adult* and *change*. Provide guidance to ensure that they talk about what they can do now that they could not do when they were a baby.

Page 60 Activity 1
a Learners could use the photographs they have brought to school of themselves as a baby to help them draw themselves.
b Accept appropriate answers, such as talk, walk, run and feed myself.

Page 60 Activity 2 Before they start, talk as a class about the things that toddlers can do, such as beginning to walk, playing with toys and feeding themselves.

 ICT links

Learners could use a camera to take photographs of themselves (selfies) or of their talk partner. They can then compare these with photographs of themselves when they were a baby or toddler.

Further activities

- Ask learners to complete Workbook page 37: Growing and changing.
- Create a human timeline in the classroom, from baby to adult. Ask learners to place their photographs in the appropriate place. (Don't forget to ask learners to put their names on the back of photos, so that they can be returned to the right learners later.)
- Give learners a range of items, such as a nappy, baby cup, straw, pen and book. Ask them to sort the items into groups according to who would use or wear them: a baby, toddler or themselves.
- Give learners a range of clothes to choose the ones that will fit, for example, a baby doll. They could also sort clothes into groups: for a baby, toddler or themselves. A similar activity could be carried out with toys. Make sure that learners explain their choices.

 ICT links

Learners could take photographs or a short video clip of themselves or each other role-playing being a baby, toddler, child, teenager and adult to show the differences as they grow older.

Assessment ideas

The ICT activity could be used as an assessment opportunity where learners show that they understand how humans change from a baby to elderly person through role-playing and videoing each other. They could share the video with other learners and say which stage they are role-playing, such as a teenager.

Success criteria

While completing the activities, assess and record learners who can:

- talk about the idea that humans have babies (offspring) and describe how babies change and grow into adults
- answer questions about growing up through observation
- make comparisons between babies, toddlers and children.

 Workbook answers

Page 37 Growing and changing

For example:

A baby can sit up, cry and laugh.

A toddler can walk, begin to feed himself or herself and say some words.

A school child can dress and feed himself or herself, read and write.

A teenager can go out on their own with friends, have a paper round and cook for themselves.

An adult can go to work and drive a car.

An older person can look after grandchildren, show children how to do things, and read them stories.

Growing up

 Learner's Book
pages 61–62

 Workbook
page 38

 Digital Resource

Objectives

- Know that humans and animals produce offspring which grow into adults. (1Bh5)
- Know about the need for a healthy diet, including the right types of food and water. (1Bh3)
- Try to answer questions by collecting evidence through observation. (1Ep1)
- Make comparisons. (1Eo4)

Background information

The activities on page 61 of the Learner's Book develop learners' understanding of the changes that take place in humans, from being a baby through to adulthood. Key to this understanding is focusing on learners observing changes between humans at different stages of their life cycle. You can support learners by encouraging them to bring in and use photographs of themselves and their family. You can also use pictures and video clips of people at different stages of life. At each stage, work with the positives; in other words things that they *can* do, while acknowledging those things that they are unable to do. When discussing elderly people, make sure that learning is not focused only on negatives, but also the positives of experience, time for others, and so on.

The activities on page 62 of the Learner's Book develop learners' knowledge of different food groups, beginning with fruit and vegetables. Vegetables and fruit provide important minerals and vitamins such as vitamin C (found in citrus fruits) which help to fight off illness. Carrots contain vitamin A which is good for healthy eyes. Fruit and vegetables are also high-fibre foods that help the digestive system, for example, eating beans and broccoli helps to prevent constipation. Ask learners if they have heard about *food groups*. Ask them what they know about different food groups, and talk about why fruit and vegetables are important.

Be careful

Throughout this part of the unit, be aware of learners who have food intolerances, both in discussions and when offering foods for tasting.

Starter activity suggestions

- Use photographs brought in by learners, as well as the pictures and the Unit 1 digital resource slideshow, slide 6: Growing up, to compare the similarities and differences between humans at different stages of life.

  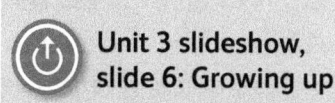 **Unit 3 slideshow, slide 6: Growing up**

- Ask learners to say what they are looking forward to when they are a teenager, adult and elderly person.
- Learners could create a family timeline, from babies to great grandparents, using their photographs. Keep a set of pictures for those learners who are unable to bring photographs to school.
- Bring a range of fruit and vegetables to school for learners to look at, compare and taste.
- Ask learners to name the different fruit and vegetables. Teach the names of those that they do not know. Use the term *food group* with learners. Explain that fruit and vegetables are a group of food that are good for people.
- Ask learners to sort the fruit and vegetables, initially into categories of their own choice.
- Give learners time to explore the outside of fruits and vegetables. They could draw, paint or photograph their favourites. Then cut fruit and vegetables open so that learners can compare the outside and inside, as well as record what they look like. Use vocabulary such as *skin*, *seeds*, *stringy*, *flesh*, *segments* and *juice*.
- Have tasting sessions with the fruit and vegetables. Encourage learners to use words associated with food, such as *sweet*, *sour*, *crunchy*, *soft* and *hard*.

Activity notes and answers

Page 61 Activity 1 Encourage learners to write words or sentences to describe what they can do as a child, such as run, write, go to school and ride a bike.

Page 61 Activity 2

a Encourage learners to think about teenagers that they know. They could include examples such as:
They go to 'big school', walk home by themselves, play basketball and have a mobile phone.

b Look at their pictures for evidence of changes, such as height, what they are wearing and doing.

c Learners could write words or sentences, such as *eat, walk, sleep, play, read and watch TV.*

Page 61 Activity 3 Learners could write words as an individual list, or as one created by a group or the whole class. It could include examples such as *drive a car, have a job and have a family.*

Page 61 Activity 4 This could be a group or whole class activity to elicit their ideas about elderly people. Encourage them to draw from their own experience of family members and others that they know. Ask them to think about what is special about the older people that they know, such as that they are able to spend time with children, read to them and take them places.

Fruit and vegetables

 Activity notes and answers

Page 62 Activity 1 Give learners access to the names of fruits and vegetables so that they can name them. Provide pictures to help them, if necessary.

Page 62 Challenge yourself! Learners could use the photograph on page 62 of the Learner's Book, or they can choose from the selection that you provided for learners to observe and taste. Learners could try new fruit and vegetables at home, or bring them from home and talk about their favourite.

Further activities

- Ask learners to complete Workbook page 38: Fruit and vegetables.

- Ask learners to complete the Unit 3 digital resource PCM1: Different ages.

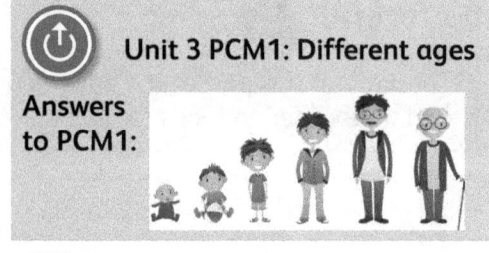
Unit 3 PCM1: Different ages

Answers to PCM1:

- Learners could create their own photo album in their books, each photograph being labelled with the correct life stage: baby, toddler, and so on. The photographs could have captions saying what the person in the photograph can do at their stage of life.

- Create a food display, with favourite fruit and vegetable pictures.

- Make a fruit and vegetable stall role-play area to use for naming, weighing and using coins to buy fruit and vegetables.

Success criteria

While completing the activities, assess and record learners who can:

- tell someone that humans have babies which change and grow into adults
- tell someone that fruit and vegetables are good foods to eat
- look at photographs or video clips and describe how humans change from a baby to an elderly person
- compare similarities and differences between people of different ages.

Workbook answers

Page 38 Fruit and vegetables

1 a grapes, sweet potato, okra, banana, carrots

2 a can of cola
  b biscuit
  c chocolate

3 They help to keep us healthy.

Bread, rice, pasta and potatoes

 Learner's Book
pages 63–64

 Workbook
page 39

 Digital Resource

Objectives

- Know about the need for a healthy diet, including the right types of food and water. (1Bh3)
- Model and communicate ideas in order to share, explain and develop them. (1Eo6)

Background information

The activities on pages 63 and 64 of the Learner's Book develop learners' knowledge of two key food groups: carbohydrates (bread, rice, pasta and potatoes) and dairy food.

Carbohydrates such as pasta, bread, rice and potatoes are important because they are an energy source that allows us to do everyday things, as well as playing sport or running. Fibre from carbohydrates, such as potato skins, is important for bowel movement and reducing constipation. They also help us to feel full, and therefore less likely to eat more.

Dairy foods such as milk, cheese and yoghurt are especially important in young children's diet, but also for older children and adults. Like carbohydrates, they are a source of energy, of protein, vitamins and minerals. One mineral, calcium, is important for building healthy bones and teeth.

When discussing food groups, help learners to realise that choosing the right foods, as well as not eating too many sweets, cakes, biscuits or drinking sugary drinks, is important to make sure that they grow up healthy. Explain that the term *balanced meal* encourages people to choose from the range of food groups, so that we eat all of the right nutrients that the body needs to be healthy.

Starter activity suggestions

- Bring a range of pasta, rice, bread and potatoes to the classroom for learners to explore and, where appropriate, sample. Ask the class to share experiences of how these foods are eaten, such as cooked, with sauces or for making sandwiches.
- Explain to learners that pasta, bread, rice and potatoes are foods that give us energy. They enable us to do things. Ask learners which ones are their favourite.
- Have tasting sessions with different carbohydrates, such as pasta salad, sweet potato and different kinds of breads. Ask the learners, *Which ones do you prefer?* Encourage learners to discuss the different tastes and textures with each other. Include something that learners perhaps have not encountered. Encourage them to try something new. Take a class vote on who did and did not like the 'mystery' food.
- Ask them to draw a meal from the previous day and label the fruit, vegetables, pasta, rice, bread and potatoes.
- Give learners different kinds of pasta (including different shapes) and ask them to make up names for them, such as pasta twists, pasta bows and pasta tubes.

Activity notes and answers

Page 63 Activity 1

a Learners' answers will depend on types of pasta eaten in their community, as well as other foods eaten with pasta. Provide some examples if pasta does not form an important part of their food culture, such as spaghetti with meatballs and tomato sauce.

b Learners could write a caption to go alongside their plate, describing why pasta is good for them.

Page 63 Activity 2

a and b Learners show their plates to other learners. They should be able to talk about pasta being a food that gives them energy, for example to move around, play and do school work.

Dairy foods

 Activity notes and answers

Page 64 Activity 1

a Learners could choose from named pictures or from packets of labelled dairy foods.

b Learners could draw or tell someone else about what they eat dairy foods with.

c Learners could draw or cut out pictures of dairy foods that they eat, and label them. Ask learners to say why these foods are important to eat as part of their diet.

Further activities

- Ask learners to complete Workbook page 39: Food groups.

- Challenge learners to recognise where we combine the food groups, such as tomato sauce and pasta, stir-fried vegetables and rice, a cheese sandwich, or flatbreads with vegetable curry. Ask them to draw food combinations on a paper plate, or stick pictures of food combinations on the plate.

- Using pictures, packets of food or toy food, learners could create their own plate of food from the different food groups.

- Ask learners to make dough models of different foods and paint them, to be placed on a plate.

- Display the Unit 3 digital resource slideshow, slide 7: Healthy food. Use it to discuss what a balanced plate of food might contain. Ask the learners, *Which foods would you choose?*

 Unit 3 slideshow, slide 7: Healthy food

Answers to slide 7:

a This will depend on personal preferences, but encourage learners to think about healthy food from different food groups.

b Focus on the idea that sugary food can be bad for teeth, although it does provide energy.

 ICT links

Ask learners to make their favourite milkshake using fruit. They could take photographs of making the milkshake. They could then use their photos to create a recipe card or book. Alternatively, they could video each other while explaining how to make a milkshake.

Success criteria

While completing the activities, assess and record learners who can:

- talk about why we need a healthy diet and what foods to eat to stay healthy

- make food models and model plates of food and explain to others why it is a healthy plate of food.

 Workbook answers

Page 39 Food groups

1 Learners should draw appropriate food on each plate:

a dairy

b bread, rice, pasta and potatoes

c meat, fish, eggs and beans.

2 Learners' own choices.

Meat, fish, eggs and beans

 Learner's Book
pages 65–66

 Workbook
page 40

 Digital Resource

Objectives

- Know about the need for a healthy diet, including the right types of food and water. (1Bh3)
- Make comparisons. (1Eo4)
- Model and communicate ideas in order to share, explain and develop them. (1Eo6)

Background information

The activities on page 65 of the Learner's Book continue to develop learners' knowledge of different food groups, focusing on meat, fish, eggs and beans. This group is the protein group of foods that are important for building tissues, cells and muscles, as well as providing antibodies to fight illness.

Water is essential for life. Our bodies are about 60 per cent water, and humans cannot live more than a few days without water. We need water to carry out a range of functions, including digesting food and getting rid of waste through sweat and urine. Blood, which contains a lot of water, carries oxygen to all the cells in our bodies. Without oxygen, those tiny cells would die and our bodies would stop working. Humans need more water when they exercise or when it is hot. If we feel thirsty, it is the body telling us that we are already dehydrated and need to drink fluid, such as water and milk. Alternatively, we could eat fruit or vegetables which contain water, such as melon and tomatoes.

Starter activity suggestions

- Display the Unit 3 digital resource slideshow, slide 7: Healthy food. Use it to recap on the different food groups that learners have learnt about so far. Talk about the meat, fish, eggs and beans group, explaining why they are an important part of a healthy diet. Compare the groups. Ask the learners, *Should we eat more of this group than fruit and vegetables or pasta, rice, potatoes and bread? Why or why not?*

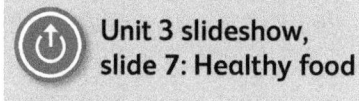 Unit 3 slideshow, slide 7: Healthy food

- Show learners pictures of different kinds of meat, fish, eggs and beans, particularly those eaten in your local area or country. Ask learners if they recognise any that they eat at home, and which ones they like.

- Ask learners to think about what they have already learnt about what living things need to stay alive. Guide them towards focusing on food and water. Ask learners to talk to a partner about why they think the body needs water, and how they know when they need to have a drink.

- Use the idea that our bodies are about 60 per cent water for a class demonstration. Ask a learner to come to the front. Using blue paper and beginning at the feet, gradually cover the learner's body with the paper until it reaches just over halfway up their body. This helps to illustrate to learners how much of the body is water and how important water is to humans. Learners will not have covered percentages yet, so a visualisation of this sort is very helpful. Make sure learners understand that their bodies are not simply filled with water up to this line though!

 ## Activity notes and answers

Page 65 Activity 1

Fish plate – sardines, salmon
Eggs plate – duck eggs, hen eggs

Meat plate – brown meat, chicken
Beans plate – lentils, chickpeas, red kidney beans

Page 65 Activity 2

a Check that learners have included their favourite foods from the protein food group.
b Check that learners have added some vegetables.
c Check that learners have added something from the pasta, rice and potato group.

Ask learners, *Do you think it would be a good idea to leave out one of the food groups? Why or why not?* Use the term *balanced meal* to help emphasise that a balanced meal has some food from each group.

To support this activity, give learners the photocopiable page: Food swap, on page 157 of this Teacher's Pack to complete.

Answers:
Accept any suggestions from the main food groups: fruit and vegetables; dairy foods; bread, rice, pasta and potatoes; meat, fish, eggs and beans. Accept water, milk or fruit juice.

Water

 Activity notes and answers

Page 66 Activity 1
Example answers:
a Listen to learners talking. They might say that they feel thirsty when their mouths are dry, or when they find it hard to swallow or eat certain foods.
b Listen to learners. They might talk about being hot, running or doing sports when they have not drunk a lot of water.
c Accept appropriate drawings (for example, running, eating lots of salty foods) to show what makes them thirsty. Ask learners to add a sentence explaining their picture.

Further activities

- Ask learners to complete Workbook page 40: Water diary.

- Ask learners to keep a diary showing what they drink each day and how much they drink, such as how many glasses. (This diary can be used as part of the work on page 67 of the Learner's Book.) Give learners time to share their diaries and what they have found out about each other. Ask: *Do you think that you drink enough water or other fluids?*

- Ask learners to think about how they could drink more water or milk, or eat more fruit and vegetables.

- Give learners samples of different fruit and vegetables. Ask them to decide which one has the most water and would be good to eat to make sure they get plenty of water.

 ICT links

Ask learners to vote for their favourite drink and create a class pictogram. You could use a data package to create the pictogram on the interactive whiteboard or on a computer.

Success criteria

While completing the activities, assess and record learners who can:

- say why meat, fish, eggs and beans are good to eat and say why it is important to drink water
- compare different fruits and vegetables and say which one is best to eat when you are thirsty
- communicate what they know to others.

 Workbook answers
Page 40 Water diary
1 a Friday
  b Thursday
  c strawberries
  d Tuesday

Water diary

 Learner's Book
pages 67–68

 Workbook
page 41

 Digital Resource

Objectives

- Know about the need for a healthy diet, including the right types of food and water. (1Bh3)
- Explore and observe in order to collect evidence (measurements and observations) to answer questions. (1Eo1)
- Record stages in work. (1Eo3)

Background information

The activity on page 67 of the Learner's Book reinforces the need to drink water as part of a healthy diet. By keeping a water diary each day for a week, the learners are collecting and recording data (which are important science skills), as well as looking at the data to draw conclusions. The learners could measure their intake of water using non-standard measures, such as how many glasses of water (or milk) they drink each day. By keeping the diary at school, you can compare days. You could then discuss how they can, for example, improve on the amount they drank on the first day of the week. If learners drink juice or fizzy drinks, discuss that these can contain a lot of sugar which can be bad for our teeth, and are not as good as water or milk. Encourage them to think about 'swapping' fizzy drinks for water or milk, as well as taking regular breaks to have a drink throughout the day.

The activities on page 68 aim to consolidate and apply what learners know about why fruit is important as part of a healthy diet through making fruit kebabs. Challenge learners to think about which fruit has the most water and which fruits they will use to make a rainbow kebab.

Starter activity suggestions

- Start the lesson with everyone drinking a paper cup full of water, and then have regular water breaks throughout the day.
- Make a water diary of your own. Show it to the class and ask them questions about how much water you drank during a week. Ask them to say whether they think you drank enough water, which day you drank the least, which day you drank the most, and so on. It would help learners if this was a pictorial diary, showing the number of glasses of water that you drank each day.
- Make a class pictogram to show how many children drank 1–8 glasses of water on one particular day of the week.
- Bring a fruit kebab that you have made to class. Ask learners to discuss, with their partners or in a group, how they think you made the kebab.

 ## Activity notes and answers

Page 67 Activity 1

a Learners keep a water diary over a week. This could be in the form of a simple table or a mini-booklet where each page is one day, with learners recording what they have been drinking and eating on each page. Diaries usually work better if learners are given a specific time during the day to complete them. This works well as a whole class session.

b Learners could write a sentence or draw a picture to show how they can make sure they drink enough water.

Fruit kebabs

 Activity notes and answers

Page 68 Activity 1 You could, over the course of a day or two, work with small groups so that they can make their kebabs. You can let them use pre-cut pieces of fruit or cut up fruit themselves for their kebabs. Emphasise safe cutting methods if they are cutting up the fruit themselves.

a To plan their kebab, learners can draw, or cut and stick in pictures, of what they will put on their kebab. Encourage learners to use different fruits. Ask them to create a simple pattern, such as grape or kiwi fruit. You could ask them to use as many different colours or textures of fruit as possible. This challenges them to think about what they are using, rather than just putting anything on their kebab.

b Make sure that you discuss hygiene rules, such as washing hands before handling food and tying hair back.

c Learners could draw, or take a photo, to record what their kebab looks like or the steps they took to make it.

Page 68 Challenge yourself! Learners could share a recipe or picture of a fruit kebab they made at home with the rest of the class.

Further activities

- Ask learners to complete Workbook page 41: Down the snakes and up the ladders!
- Ask learners to complete the Unit 3 digital resource PCM2: Getting more water.

 Unit 3 PCM2: Getting more water

Answers to PCM2:
1 a milk, water, tomato, melon, eggplant, pineapple, pepper, water, strawberry
2 For example: *We need to drink water to stay healthy.*

- Learners could find out and bring information to school about how many glasses of water other members of their family drink during the day.
- Make a class pictogram of favourite fruits for kebabs.
- Learners could share and try out someone else's recipe for a fruit kebab.
- Ask learners to design and make a vegetable kebab.

 ICT links

Learners could take photographs of each other making fruit kebabs. They can then use them to make a recipe card of how to make a kebab. Use apps such as Pic collage, so that learners can make their own fruit kebab collage. Learners could share these on the school website.

Success criteria

While completing the activities, assess and record learners who can:

- say how they can drink more water and milk and why it is good for them
- collect measurements to find out how much water they drink in a week
- record how much water they drank using a chart, and how they made their kebabs by drawing pictures, writing sentences or taking photographs.

 Workbook answers

Page 41 Down the snakes and up the ladders!

1 Encourage learners to play the game in pairs. Provide support for those learners who need help with reading the gameboard.

Tooth decay

Learner's Book
pages 69–71

Workbook
page 42

Objectives

- Know about the need for a healthy diet, including the right types of food and water. (1Bh3)
- Try to answer questions by collecting evidence through observation. (1Ep1)
- Explore and observe in order to collect evidence (measurements and observations) to answer questions. (1Eo1)
- Record stages in work. (1Eo3)
- Make comparisons. (1Eo4)

Background information

The activities on pages 69 and 70 of the Learner's Book develop learners' knowledge of the effect of sweet, sugary foods on dental health. Sweets and sugary foods are less healthy than other foods. Not only do they lack important minerals and vitamins, but they also can lead to tooth decay and poor dental health. The mouth contains some unhealthy bacteria which feed on the sugars that we eat. This creates an acid which destroys the shiny outer covering of teeth (enamel). This is known as *tooth decay*. Tooth decay can lead to cavities (holes in the teeth), toothache and sensitivity to sweet, hot or cold foods or drinks. If left untreated, tooth decay can result in teeth having to be removed, gum disease and bad breath.

To avoid tooth decay, we need to reduce sugar intake, brush teeth regularly, eat dairy foods to strengthen teeth, and drink milk and water rather than sugary drinks and juices (which are acidic). This part of the unit is an excellent opportunity to invite a dentist or dental nurse to talk to the class, or for a visit to a dental surgery.

The activities on page 71 revisit and revise some of the ideas presented in this unit.

Starter activity suggestions

- Visit a dental surgery, or invite a dentist or dental nurse to talk to the class. Encourage the learners to ask questions.
- Ask learners why teeth are important and what they think would happen if they did not look after their teeth. Collect their ideas.
- Ask learners what they think would happen if they only ate sweet things and did not clean their teeth. Collect their ideas.
- Show learners a range of dental hygiene products, such as toothbrushes, tooth paste, interdental brushes or floss. Ask learners if they know what they are, what they are used for, and so on.
- Recap the different food groups and discuss which foods are good for teeth.
- Give learners a mirror each, so that they can observe their teeth. Talk about the different teeth and their functions.

Activity notes and answers

Page 69 Talk partners Listen to talk partners and use their discussions to find out what they know about dental hygiene.
Example answers:
a Black, rotten, broken
b Because of eating too many sweet things, drinking fizzy drinks or juices, not brushing teeth.
c Eat fruit, vegetables and cheese, drink water and milk, brush and floss teeth regularly, and visit the dentist.

Look after your smile

 Activity notes and answers

Page 70 Activity 1 Learners use a mirror to observe their teeth. Scaffold learning here by encouraging learners to slow down, observe carefully, count their teeth, look for teeth that are different shapes and sizes, and whether the teeth on the top row are the same as those on the bottom row. Do use words such as *incisors* and *molars*; there is no reason why learners should not be exposed to these words, and learners may already know them.

Page 70 Activity 2
Answers:
a Milk, toothpaste, cheese, toothbrush
b As well as drawing the milk, toothpaste, cheese and toothbrush, ask learners to think of other pictures they could add, such as water, dentist, dental floss, carrots and apples.

Page 70 Challenge yourself! Encourage learners to think about their own dental hygiene and what they could do to improve it. Give learners access to books, video clips, and so on to find out about what dentists do.

What have you learnt about living and growing?

 Activity notes and answers

Page 71 Activity 1
Answers:
Alive – flowers, cat
Never been alive – rocks, keys

Page 71 Activity 2
Answer:
d cake

Further activities

- Ask learners to complete Workbook page 42: Look after your teeth.
- Create a display of photographs of learners in the class. Make sure that each one is smiling. Around the photographs, you can use, for example, speech bubbles for learners to write how they keep their teeth healthy.
- Give learners pictures of food and dental hygiene items to sort into things that are good for teeth and things that are not good.
- Ask learners to create a set of pictures to show how to look after teeth.
- Create a class poem about teeth. Each pair decides on something that teeth do, for example:
  What do our teeth do?
  Our teeth eat
  Our teeth chew
  Our teeth bite
  Our teeth shine
  So, look after your teeth.

 ICT links
Working in pairs, learners could make a short video to show how to clean teeth.
Give learners access to interactive activities on the computer which teach about dental hygiene.

Success criteria

While completing the activities, assess and record learners who can:

- talk about foods that are not good for teeth and that help to keep teeth healthy
- look at their teeth to answer questions
- observe decayed teeth and say why they are like this
- draw things that help to keep teeth healthy
- make comparisons between teeth.

 Workbook answers

Page 42 Look after your teeth

1 a Pictures could show, for example, brushing teeth twice a day; drinking water and milk.
  b Check that learners' sentences make sense.

Assessment ideas

- Ask learners to self-assess using the 'What can you remember?' checklist on page 71 of the Learner's Book, as well as the self-assessment table on page 43 of the Workbook.
- Ask learners to complete Quiz 1 on pages 72–73 in the Learner's Book. This provides the opportunity to recap as a class some of the ideas from this unit.

Quiz 1: Biology

Answers:

1 Check that the plant has flower, leaf, stem and roots in the correct positions.

2 water, air, light

3 seed – **c**
  seed with shoot – **d**
  seedling – **b**
  plant – **a**

4 Check that all body parts (nose, ear, mouth, arm, leg, eyes, arm, ankle, neck) have been correctly labelled.

5 **a** horse – foal
  b duck – duckling
  c human – baby
  d cat – kitten
  e sheep – lamb

6 Check that learners have included the following: fruit and vegetables; a choice from meat, fish, eggs and beans; a choice from bread, rice, pasta and potatoes; dairy produce; water or milk as a drink.

7 **a** tree – blackbird
  b rock – beetle
  c desert – camel

8 baby – **b**
  toddler – **c**
  child – **a**
  teenager – **d**
  adult – **f**
  elderly person – **e**

Unit 4 Material properties

Objectives overview

Learning objective	Objective code	Learner's Book pages	Teacher's Pack pages	Workbook pages	Digital Resource Pack
Chemistry: Material properties					
Use senses to explore and talk about different materials.	1Cp1	74, 75, 76, 77, 78, 79, 80, 81, 82, 83, 84, 85, 86, 87	91, 92, 93, 94, 95, 96, 97, 98, 99, 100, 101, 102, 103, 104	44, 45, 46, 47, 48, 49, 50	Unit 4 slides 3, 7
Identify the characteristics of different materials.	1Cp2	76, 77, 78, 79, 80, 81, 82, 83, 84, 85, 86, 87, 90, 91, 92, 93	93, 94, 95, 96, 97, 98, 99, 100, 101, 102, 103, 104, 107, 108, 109, 110, 111	44, 45, 46, 47, 48, 49, 50, 51, 52, 53, 54, 55	Unit 4 slides 5, 6, 7 PCM1, video clip
Recognise and name common materials.	1Cp3	74, 75, 80, 81, 82, 83, 84, 85, 86, 87, 88, 89	91, 92, 97, 98, 99, 100, 101, 102, 103, 104, 105, 106	44, 48, 49, 50, 51, 52, 53, 54, 56	Unit 4 slides 3, 4, 5, 6, 7, PCM2 , interactive activity
Sort objects into groups based on the properties of their materials	1Cp4	74, 75, 76, 77, 80, 81, 82, 83, 84, 85, 87, 88, 89	91, 92, 93, 94, 97, 98, 99, 100, 101, 102, 103, 104, 105, 106	45, 46, 48, 49, 50	Unit 4 slides 4, 5
Scientific enquiry: Ideas and evidence					
Try to answer questions by collecting evidence through observation.	1Ep1	76, 77, 88, 89, 91, 92, 93	93, 94, 105, 106, 107, 108, 109, 110, 111	45, 46, 47, 48, 49, 50, 51, 52, 53, 55, 56	Unit 4 slides 5, 6
Scientific enquiry: Plan investigative work					
Ask questions and contribute to discussions about how to seek answers.	1Ep2				
Make predictions.	1Ep3	90, 91, 92, 93	107, 108, 109, 110, 111		

Learning objective	Objective code	Learner's Book pages	Teacher's Pack pages	Workbook pages	Digital Resource Pack
Decide what to do to try to answer a science question.	1Ep4	88, 89, 91, 93	105, 106, 107, 108, 109, 110, 111	53	
Scientific enquiry: Obtain and present evidence					
Explore and observe in order to collect evidence (measurements and observations) to answer questions.	1Eo1	76, 77, 90, 91, 93	93, 94, 107, 108, 109, 110, 111	44, 45, 48, 50, 52, 53, 55	PCM1
Suggest ideas and follow instructions.	1Eo2	80, 81, 84	97, 98, 101, 102		
Record stages in work.	1Eo3	76, 77, 78, 81, 83, 84, 86, 87, 89, 90, 91, 93	93, 94, 95, 96, 97, 98, 99, 100, 101, 102, 103, 104, 105, 106, 107, 108, 109, 110, 111		
Scientific enquiry: Consider evidence and approach					
Make comparisons.	1Eo4	74, 75, 76, 77, 78, 79, 80, 81, 82, 83, 84, 85, 87, 88, 89	91, 92, 93, 94, 95, 96, 97, 98, 99, 100, 101, 102, 103, 104, 105, 106	44, 45, 46, 47, 48, 49, 50, 51, 53	
Compare what happened with predictions.	1Eo5	91, 93	107, 108, 109, 110, 111	55	
Model and communicate ideas in order to share, explain and develop them.	1Eo6	79	95, 96		

Feeling materials

 Learner's Book
pages 74–75

 Workbook
page 44

 Digital Resource

Objectives

- Use senses to explore and talk about different materials. (1Cp1)
- Recognise and name common materials. (1Cp3)
- Sort objects into groups based on the properties of their materials (1Cp4)
- Make comparisons. (1Eo4)

Background information

The aim of the activities on pages 74 and 75 of the Learner's Book is to elicit what learners already know about materials. They allow you to find out if learners recognise different materials and which ones they can name, so that you can build on their understanding. You can also find out if learners can distinguish between the object and the material. Do they know, for example, that rulers can be made from different materials and that they are not always made from wood or plastic?

Eliciting learners' ideas at the beginning of a unit provides you with an opportunity to assess what learners already know, and whether or not they require additional experiences. You can then ensure that they are secure in their ideas before moving on. Do not worry if they do not remember the words immediately; there will be other opportunities in this unit for repetition and reinforcement of key scientific vocabulary. Some learners might recognise, for example, wood in one object, but not in another if it looks very different. The aim of this unit is for learners to engage in a wide range of experiences which will develop their knowledge of materials. This will help them to confidently name and describe the properties of everyday materials.

Starter activity suggestions

- Create a collection of objects made from different materials for learners to sort according to their own criteria. At this stage, accept all answers from the learners. This will provide an opportunity to assess what they already know.

- Give learners boxes or hoops with names of materials on them, such as metal, wood, plastic and fabric. Ask learners to sort objects. Get them to work in pairs, so that they can discuss their ideas and support each other in decision making. You could create a character face with a huge mouth for each of the boxes, so that learners can sort the objects according to their materials by 'posting' the object through the mouth into the box.

- Display the Unit 4 digital resource slideshow, slide 3: Materials hunt. Use it to find out which materials learners can name. You could ask them to find objects made from these materials in the classroom.

 Unit 4 slideshow, slide 3: Materials hunt

Answers to slide 3:

notepad – paper; paperclips – metal; hat – wool; chair – wood; bricks – plastic.

 Activity notes and answers

Page 74 Talk partners

a If you find that learners do not appear to have the language to name the materials, provide them with the names and ask them to choose. Alternatively, bring the objects into the classroom so that learners can explore them using their senses, and so that you can teach them the material names.
  Answers:
  bottle (glass), pegs (wood and metal), notepad (paper), hat (wool), scooter (metal)
b Listen to learners' responses to see if they can make connections in relation to materials around the

classroom, home and the local environment. This will provide an opportunity for you to find out what they already know.

c Listen to learners, then bring the class together and ask them to share ideas. You could write their ideas in 'thought bubbles' on a wall display, along with the learner's name. This could be the starting point for a 'Materials working wall' which learners can either add to themselves, or an adult could write the ideas as the unit progresses.

Page 74 Activity 1

a Giving learners a small bag or basket for their hunt is helpful, as well as pictures or small samples of materials to match items.

b Listen to learners' ideas. You could offer them word cards to use as support, such as *shiny*, *rough*, *smooth* and *bumpy*.

c Learners could name materials orally, or place a card next to each object to name the material it is made from. Some learners might choose an object made of several materials, so challenge them to name the different materials.

What are materials?

 Activity notes and answers

Page 75 Activity 1

a Some learners might benefit from picking out all of the objects made from the same material first, then another material.

b Learners might sort according to the name of the material or the property. Accept the different ways they sort materials, as this will help you to find out whether they are sorting according to features such as shape or colour, or according to names or properties of materials, such as smooth, rough, and so on.

Page 75 Activity 2 Accept the ways in which learners sort. This provides an opportunity for assessment of where they are in their understanding of materials. Encourage learners not to say *You are wrong* to other learners, but rather *It could be that, but that is not how we sorted them, try again.* The aim is for learners to appreciate that others might have different ideas but which might also work.

Further activities

● Ask learners to complete Workbook page 44: Materials all around us.

● Ask learners to bring different objects from home (with permission from parents or carers) to add to a 'Materials' science table. Make sure that their names are on the objects. Learners could sort and group the objects according to different materials. Ask learners to name the different materials on the table, using name cards. Leave sticky notes so that learners can record how they have sorted.

● Have a photo hunt for materials inside the classroom and outside in the school grounds, with each child taking a photograph of the material of their choice. Place the photographs on a working wall or perhaps in a big book on materials.

Success criteria

While completing the activities, assess and record learners who can:

● use their sense of touch to explore different materials

● recognise and name objects and the materials they are made from

● sort objects made from different materials into groups

● compare objects that are made from similar and different materials.

 Workbook answers

Page 44 Materials all around us

1 a material

b objects

2 Check learners' drawings and labels.

Soft textures

 Learner's Book
pages 76–77

 Workbook
page 45

Objectives

- Use senses to explore and talk about different materials. (1Cp1)
- Identify the characteristics of different materials. (1Cp2)
- Sort objects into groups based on the properties of their materials. (1Cp4)
- Try to answer questions by collecting evidence through observation. (1Ep1)
- Explore and observe in order to collect evidence (measurements and observations) to answer questions. (1Eo1)
- Record stages in work. (1Eo3)
- Make comparisons. (1Eo4)

Background information

The activities on pages 76 and 77 of the Learner's Book develop learners' ability to use their senses to explore different materials. Key words to model with learners are *materials* and *texture* (what a material feels like). This will ensure that they not only become familiar with these terms, but gradually begin to own and use them in their dialogue with their peers and adults.

Include *compare*, *similar* and *different* in the terms that you model. They are important words in science and help to focus observations. When learners can correctly apply these words in different contexts, you can be confident that they have mastered the ideas behind them.

Starter activity suggestions

- Give learners materials that are soft, as well as objects such soft toys, blankets and clothing to feel the texture. This will help them to learn from first-hand experience what *soft* feels like.
- Ask learners to bring into class (with permission) anything that they have at home that they think is soft.
- If you have photographs of learners, place them around a display board about materials. Use thought or speech bubbles and write (or let learners write) their favourite material that is soft to touch.
- Create an interactive display of objects that are soft for learners to explore and make comparisons between textures.
- Place swatches of different materials for learners to sort into soft/not soft.

Activity notes and answers

Page 76 Activity 1

Check that learners choose appropriate soft materials for this activity. You could give learners the photocopiable page: Soft materials (with a rabbit template), on page 158 of this Teacher's Pack, to complete.

Page 76 Talk partners

a Listen to learners as they answer the questions about what things are made from soft materials in their homes.

b Ask learners to talk to their partners about pictures that they have drawn, so that they articulate their ideas before writing sentences.

c Ask learners to read out the sentences they have written to their talk partner.

93

Other textures

 Activity notes and answers

Page 77 Activity 1

a Listen to learners discussing textures of materials.

b and **c**   Observe the choices learners make and ask them to name the textures they choose.

d Learners should use the correct vocabulary linked to the materials chosen.

Page 77 Challenge yourself! Learners could create a mini-collection of things that are soft, slippery, bumpy and smooth. Challenge them to choose things that would fit into a small box.

Further activities

- Ask learners to complete Workbook page 45: It feels soft!
- If learners make mini-collections, they could swap their collection with someone else and sort their collection into the different textures.
- Give learners key texture words to learn how to spell. This could be a home-school science activity.
- Ask learners to make their own texture board by using card and sticking on different textures for other learners to touch and name.
- Place materials of different textures in a bag. Ask learners to pick out objects which have the same texture, using only the sense of touch.

 ICT links

Learners could use a computer app such as Pic collage to record different objects made of materials with specific textures.

Success criteria

While completing the activities, assess and record learners who can:

- use their senses to explore materials
- name different textures of materials
- sort materials into groups of different textures
- answer questions about materials through using their senses
- explore and observe materials to answer questions about what texture they have
- record their work using pictures, sentences and photographs
- compare the textures of different materials.

 Workbook answers

Page 45 It feels soft!

1 Accept appropriate drawings, which might include: cushion, soft toy, blanket, scarf, animal fur, fluffy socks, and so on.

2 Check learners' sentences.

Texture lolly game

Learner's Book
pages 78–79

Workbook
pages 46–47

Objectives

- Use senses to explore and talk about different materials. (1Cp1)
- Identify the characteristics of different materials. (1Cp2)
- Record stages in work. (1Eo3)
- Make comparisons. (1Eo4)
- Model and communicate ideas in order to share, explain and develop them. (1Eo6)

Background information

The activities on page 78 of the Learner's Book provide an opportunity for learners to use their knowledge of the textures of different materials to create a simple game to play with their talk partner. The aim is for learners to think about different textures and choose materials with a range of textures to stick to each of their lolly sticks. Of importance here is that learners work independently to choose the textures that they want to put on the lolly sticks, using their senses to make decisions about which one to use and to make sure that they have a variety. Do make your own set so that learners can see how to make them and how to play the game.

The activities on page 79 of the Learner's Book challenge learners to pair up materials in terms of their opposites, such as *rough* and *smooth*, *hard* and *soft*. Throughout these activities, the emphasis is on learners using knowledge about materials and using the correct scientific words. Scaffold language for those learners who need support to access specific vocabulary.

Starter activity suggestions

- Show the class your set of lolly sticks and demonstrate the game from Activity 2 on Learner's Book page 78 with several learners. Then ask for a pair to show the rest of the class how to play the game. The game is straightforward. Learners ask their partner to pick a lolly stick with a particular material that has a specific characteristic, such as soft or rough. Their partner has to find it. If they get it right, they score a point. You may need to teach learners how to keep score.

- Provide a wide range of materials for learners to choose from. Encourage them to make some of the lolly sticks in their game challenging, so that their partner really has to think. For example, it might have two sets of textures.

- Discuss with the class how they could write down the scores for the game.

- Discuss the word *opposite* with learners. Ask them, *What do you think the word opposite means?* Give examples of opposites such as *hard* and *soft, wet* and *dry, shiny* and *dull.* Ask them to choose a material, feel its texture (such as *smooth*) and then find the opposite texture (such as a material that is *rough* or *bumpy*).

Activity notes and answers

Page 78 Activity 1 Check that learners have correctly identified the texture and have written it on the other side of the lolly stick to the materials they have stuck onto the stick.

Page 78 Activity 2 Observe learners playing the game, scoring and swapping over so that they each have a turn.

Opposites

 Activity notes and answers

Page 79 Activity 1
Example answers:
a hard – rock; soft – towels
b rough – bark; smooth – plastic ruler
c transparent – window; not see-through – brick

Page 79 Talk partners
a Some learners might benefit from being given, for example, four words for which they must match the opposites. They then choose one pair of words to find these materials.
b You might create a small set of materials from which learners could choose the opposites, if you think it is too challenging for them to look around the classroom.
c Use this opportunity to observe and listen to learners to find out if they understand opposites, can find opposites in materials and can talk about this with peers while using appropriate language.

Further activities

- Ask learners to complete Workbook page 46: Material properties and Workbook page 47: Opposites.
- Create an opposites book, where learners can stick in pictures of their own selection of opposites and write what they are beside the materials.

Success criteria

While completing the activities, assess and record learners who can:
- use senses to choose and name different materials
- use their senses to say what different materials are like
- use a camera to record what they have done, or make a mini-book
- make comparisons between different materials
- show others what to do and explain what the opposites are that they have chosen.

 Workbook answers

Page 46 Material properties
1 and 2 Check that learners' drawings are appropriate.

Page 47 Opposites
1 a shiny, rigid, smooth
b dull, rough, rigid
c bendy, dull, smooth

Sorting arrows

 Learner's Book
pages 80–81

 Workbook
page 48

 Digital Resource

Objectives

- Use senses to explore and talk about different materials. (1Cp1)
- Identify the characteristics of different materials. (1Cp2)
- Recognise and name common materials. (1Cp3)
- Sort objects into groups based on the properties of their materials. (1Cp4)
- Suggest ideas and follow instructions. (1Eo2)
- Record stages in work. (1Eo3)
- Make comparisons. (1Eo4)

Background information

The activities on page 80 of the Learner's Book consolidate learners' ability to sort materials according to their properties. In this case, they use sorting arrows to place the materials on a continuum. This is more challenging than previous activities, as it demands that learners apply their understanding of properties such as bumpy and smooth. For example, they must put materials in order from most bumpy to smoothest. You will need to demonstrate this. You could use learners and put them in order from tallest to shortest, then choose objects and ask members of the class to order them.

The activities on page 81 of the Learner's Book elicit which learners can name the materials that objects are made from. This provides an opportunity to assess what learners already know about naming materials. As with all scientific language, it is important that you offer learners many different opportunities to practise using these words, so that they become confident in using them. Page 9 of this Teacher's Pack has a section on ways to teach and reinforce key language.

Starter activity suggestions

- Make a set of large arrows. Demonstrate using them with the class to order members of the class, tallest to shortest. Then apply the same approach to ordering some materials (use five materials if possible).
- Create with learners a collection of objects made from materials such as *metal, plastic, paper, wood, leather* and *fabric*. Ask learners to sort them into groups. You might begin by asking them to sort into one group of objects made from metal, then made from wood, and so on. As you do so, get them to say the word, read the word and spell out the word phonetically.
- Give learners name cards of the different types of materials. Ask them to put the cards next to objects made from the material.
- Display the Unit 4 digital resource slideshow, slide 4: Match the material to the object. Ask learners to match the name to the material that the different objects are made from.

 Unit 4 slideshow, slide 4: Match the material to the object

Answers to slide 4:

sharpener – metal; jug – plastic; T-shirt – fabric; train – wood; notepad – paper.

 Activity notes and answers

Page 80 Activity 1

a Check that learners have sorted their materials appropriately.

b Listen to learners' discussions, to find out what their reasoning is and if they agree or disagree. This will help you to know which learners are confident in their understanding of materials.

Page 80 Activity 2
a Check that learners have correctly ordered their objects from shiniest to dullest.
b Check that learners have correctly ordered their objects from bendy to not bendy (rigid).

Names of materials

 Activity notes and answers

Page 81 Activity 1
Answers:
a pan – metal; spoons – wood; bottles – glass; toy truck – plastic; soft toy – fabric; shoes – leather
b Check which pictures learners identify as ones where they do not know the name of the material. Provide guidance to help them identify the materials.

Page 81 Activity 2
a Check the objects that learners collect.
b Print out the photograph so the learners can annotate the objects with the names of the materials they are made from. Support learners by providing a word bank to copy from or write what they say.
c Check the labels for each object to make sure that learners can name the materials they are made from.

Further activities

- Ask learners to complete Workbook page 48: Materials in the kitchen.
- The class could go on a materials hunt around the school and outside, to find objects made from different materials. They could complete a simple grid and draw what they find under headings such as wood, metal and glass. Alternatively they could use a camera to take photographs.

 ICT links

Ask learners to use a camera to take photographs of objects made from different materials. They could then use the computer app Pic collage to make a collage of objects made from the same material, such as metal.

Success criteria

While completing the activities, assess and record learners who can:
- use their senses to explore and talk about different materials
- say what materials are like, such as smooth
- name common materials
- sort objects into groups based on what the materials are like, such as rough
- follow instructions on using the arrows for sorting
- take photographs of different materials
- make comparisons between different materials.

 Workbook answers

Page 48 Materials in the kitchen

1 a and b cotton – tea towel
    metal – saucepan
    wood – spoon
    plastic – water bottle
    glass – drinking glass
    wood – chopping board
    metal – cutlery
    paper – towels
2 For example:
    a metal – saucepan
    b glass – bottle
    c plastic – spoon
    d fabric – towel

Metals

 Learner's Book
pages 82–83

 Workbook
page 49

 Digital Resource

Objectives

- Use senses to explore and talk about different materials. (1Cp1)
- Identify the characteristics of different materials. (1Cp2)
- Recognise and name common materials. (1Cp3)
- Sort objects into groups based on the properties of their materials. (1Cp4)
- Record stages in work. (1Eo3)
- Make comparisons. (1Eo4)

Background information

The activities on pages 82 and 83 of the Learner's Book develop learners' knowledge of metal as a material by introducing them to the main properties (characteristics) of metal and its everyday uses. It is important for learners to know that metals can be used for more than one thing, such as to make coins, rulers, chairs, screws and hammers. Metal also has properties that make it suitable for making different objects. Metal is *strong* and can be *shiny* or *dull*, *bendy* (*flexible*) or *rigid*, *hard* and it *feels cold to the touch*. Sometimes it makes a *ringing sound* when it is hit. These properties will help learners to distinguish it from other materials. It will also help them recognise when some materials look like metal but are not, such as plastic coated to resemble metal.

As learners engage with activities to identify and sort materials made from metal, ask them to explain why they think the object is made from metal. Ask them how they know this. Ensure that they use their subject knowledge about the properties of metal and use the correct scientific words.

Starter activity suggestions

- Provide learners with a collection of objects made from different materials, including metal. Ask learners to sort them in different ways. Then ask them if they know what metal is and if they have any objects made from metal in their collection. This will provide an opportunity to determine which learners know what metal looks like.
- Ask learners to sort their collection so that they only have objects made from metal. Then ask them to work with their talk partner to find out what metal is like. For example, is it shiny or dull, or can it be both?
- Ask the class to share what they have found out about metals and write their comments. These could be recorded as part of a wall display, a big book or a table top interactive display on metal as a material.

 ## Activity notes and answers

Page 82 Activity 1

a Ask learners how they know that the object is made from metal. Listen to their responses to check that they are using, for example, *shiny*, *hard* and *cold to touch* as reasons.

Go on a metal hunt

 ## Activity notes and answers

Page 83 Activity 1

a You could give learners pieces of shiny aluminium foil and sticky tack to stick on items made from metal. It is then easy to see what the learners identify as metal. They will enjoy leaving an aluminium trail around the classroom.

b Learners can find out if the materials are metal through testing them. For example, they can tap them to see if they ring, touch them to check if they feel cold, and observe if they are dull or shiny.

Page 83 Activity 2
Answers:
a Check that objects drawn are made from metal.
b Accept, for example, metal rings; metal is shiny or dull; metal is strong; metal feels cold; metal is hard.

Further activities

● Ask learners to complete Workbook page 49: Metal objects.

● Display the Unit 4 digital resource slideshow, slide 5: Metal. Use it to repeat and reinforce learners' knowledge of the properties of metals. Also use it to make sure that learners know that metals can be different colours and can be made into different things.

 Unit 4 slideshow, slide 5: Metal

Answers to slide 5:
a Metal is usually shiny (sometimes dull), hard, it makes a ringing sound when tapped and is cold to touch.
b Learners could draw, for example, metal cutlery, door handles and keys.

● Create a class collection of objects made from metals. Learners can add to this, either by bringing safe objects from home (with permission), or by choosing from a 'box of bits' (objects made from metal) and adding them to the collection. Make sure that learners can justify their choice by explaining how they know the object is made from metal.

● Give learners access to catalogues, pictures from the internet, and so on. They can use these to create a page to illustrate a range of objects, both everyday and unusual, made from metal.

 ICT links
When learners go on a metal hunt, they could take photographs of metal objects and create a picture collage or add them to a display.

Success criteria

While completing the activities, assess and record learners who can:
● use their senses to explore and talk about metals
● say what metals are like, such as hard, shiny or dull
● say when an object is made from metal
● sort objects into groups: metal and not metal
● take photographs, draw pictures and write sentences about metals
● make comparisons between different metals.

 Workbook answers
Page 49 Metal objects
1 gloves; apple; building brick
2 hard; shiny; cold to touch

Plastic

 Learner's Book
pages 84–85

 Workbook
page 50

Objectives

- Use senses to explore and talk about different materials. (1Cp1)
- Identify the characteristics of different materials. (1Cp2)
- Recognise and name common materials. (1Cp3)
- Sort objects into groups based on the properties of their materials. (1Cp4)
- Suggest ideas and follow instructions. (1Eo2)
- Record stages in work. (1Eo3)
- Make comparisons. (1Eo4)

Background information

The activities on page 84 of the Learner's Book develop learners' knowledge of plastic as a material by introducing them to the main properties (characteristics) of plastic and its everyday uses. Plastic is one of the most versatile materials in the world. The word *plastic* comes from the Greek word *plastikos*, which means to mould or form. Plastics are materials which can have many different properties, such as hard or soft, transparent or opaque, rigid or flexible. There are hundreds of different kinds of plastics. They can be shaped into objects of different sizes, shapes and colours. They can also be made to look like other materials, such as wood or metals.

An important concept for learners to understand is that one material can be used to make more than one thing. Plastic has properties that make it suitable for making different objects. Plastic can be *strong, shiny* or *dull*, *bendy* (*flexible*) or *rigid*, *hard*, and *does not feel cold to the touch*. These properties will help learners to distinguish plastics from other materials. It will also help them to recognise that plastic can be made to look like other materials, such as metal and wood.

The activities on page 85 of the Learner's Book develop learners' understanding of wood as a material. While plastic is a man-made material, wood is a natural material that comes from trees. Wood is *strong, flexible*, and is *lighter* than other materials such as some metals. It also *lasts a long time,* so it is often used to make things that need to last, such as houses, furniture and even wooden spoons.

As learners engage with activities to identify and sort materials made from plastic or wood, ask them to explain why they think the object is made from plastic or wood. How do they know? Ensure that they use their subject knowledge about the properties of plastic and wood, and use the correct scientific words.

Starter activity suggestions

- Create collections of objects made from plastic and wood for learners to sort. These could also include items made from metal, so that learners have to compare plastic and metal, and metal and wood. Ask them: *What is similar? What is different?*
- Give learners words (either written or orally) such as *see-through* (transparent), *not see-through* (opaque), *smooth, rough, rigid* and *flexible*, to use to sort objects made from wood and plastic. This will help them to learn that these materials have many different properties.

 ## Activity notes and answers

Page 84 Activity 1

a Listen to talk partners sharing what they know about plastic. Use this to identify where they are in their learning and what the next teaching steps should be.

b and c You could place a limit on the number of objects, such as five objects per pair. Explain that they should not collect two objects that are the same. Check that the objects learners collect are made from plastic.

d Check learners' sentences describing how they know the object is made from plastic.

Page 84 Activity 2 Check that learners know that plastic can have more than property, such as transparent and rigid, smooth and flexible, not see-through and rough. For example, a plastic bottle is rigid and see-through (transparent). A pen could be made from plastic that is hard, and either see-through (transparent) or not see-through (opaque).

Wood

 Activity notes and answers

Page 85 Activity 1 Check that learners' choices of objects made from wood are correct.

Page 85 Activity 2
Answers:
a The answers to these questions will depend on the type of wood learners are accessing.
b No, the wood will not be the same.
c No, the textures will not be the same.
d Dull; does not ring like metal.

Page 85 Activity 3 Check that the criteria that learners have used to sort wooden objects are appropriate, such as *smooth*, *rough*, *bumpy*.

Further activities

- Ask learners to complete Workbook page 50: Plastic and wood.
- Show learners a video clip of metal, wood and plastic to reinforce the ideas that they can be used for many different things. Search on the internet for 'material uses' to find a video clip.
- Challenge learners to find out where paper comes from. They could carry out this research at home.
- Ask learners to create a collage of pictures of objects made from wood or plastic.
- Challenge learners to make a list that goes all the way around the classroom of objects that are made from wood, plastic and metal. Celebrate when the list completely circles the classroom.

Success criteria

While completing the activities, assess and record learners who can:
- use their senses to explore and talk about plastic
- say what plastic is like
- say when an object is made from plastic
- sort objects into groups: plastic and not plastic
- suggest ideas about the materials that objects are made from
- take photographs, draw pictures and write sentences about plastic
- make comparisons between different materials.

 Workbook answers

Page 50 Plastic and wood

1 c Check learners' drawings.
2 For example: plate, beaker, food boxes, shampoo bottle, coat hanger, pen.

Glass

 Learner's Book
pages 86–87

 Workbook
page 51

 Digital Resource

Objectives

- Use senses to explore and talk about different materials. (1Cp1)
- Identify the characteristics of different materials. (1Cp2)
- Recognise and name common materials. (1Cp3)
- Sort objects into groups based on the properties of their materials. (1Cp4)
- Record stages in work. (1Eo3)
- Make comparisons. (1Eo4)

Background information

The activities on page 86 of the Learner's Book develop learners' knowledge of glass as a material. Many materials start off quite differently to the final product. Glass begins as mainly sand with some other minerals added. It is then melted at very high temperatures. At this stage, the material can be changed to make different shapes, colours and sizes. Normally glass is *transparent* (see-through), but it can also be *translucent* (almost see-through), such as in bathroom windows. Glass is mostly used for objects that we need to be able to see through (transparent), such as windows and spectacles. It is also used, for example, for containers for storing food and for vases.

Glass can be of different thicknesses and different strengths. Thin glass is brittle and breaks easily. Glass can be made so that it shatters into small pieces, such as in car windshields.

The activities on page 87 of the Learner's Book develop learners' knowledge of fabric. The word *fabric* is often used interchangeably with the word *material*. It is important to separate the two, so that learners use them appropriately. *Materials* can be glass, metal, wood or plastic. *Fabric* is another type of material and has a range of properties. Fabric is made from fibres of, for example, wool, cotton or silk which come from living things. Other fabrics, such as polyester and nylon, are made from chemicals. Fabrics can be *rough*, *soft*, *stretchy* and *flexible*. They have the ability to *keep things warm or cool* (for example, for making clothes that we wear), or to *absorb liquids* (for example, for making cleaning cloths).

Starter activity suggestions

- Bring into class a collection of objects made from glass to show learners the variety. Include light bulbs, food containers, drinking glasses, bowls, and so on. Explain to learners that glass must be handled carefully and that if they find broken glass, they must tell an adult who will clear it up. Ask learners to discuss with partners why people use glass to make things.

- Engage learners in making a collection of different fabrics. They could bring pieces of fabric from home and sort the fabrics using their own criteria. Ask learners to sort the fabrics into different groups to check that they understand textures such as *soft*, *rough*, *silky*, *furry* and *smooth*, as well as properties such as *stretchy*.

 Activity notes and answers

Page 86 Talk partners Listen to learners discussing why the objects in the pictures are made from glass. This will provide an opportunity to access what learners already understand about glass as a material.
Example answers:
Glass jar – so you can see what is inside, so the things do not fall out, to keep them clean.
Butterfly – so it looks pretty, so the light can change the colour.
Window – so you can see through it, to keep the wind and rain out.

Page 86 Activity 1
a You could also do this activity in another part of the school or outside in the school grounds.
b Learners could draw objects either where they find them or back in the classroom.
c Ask learners to explain why they think these objects are made of glass. Correct any misconceptions.

Page 86 Challenge yourself! Give learners time to share with the class what they have found at home that is made from glass. Ask them to explain why the object is made from glass.

Fabric

 Activity notes and answers

Page 87 Activity 1
a Provide as many things as you can that are made from fabric, so that learners can access a wide range.
b Listen to learners as they compare different fabrics, either from those found around the classroom or a range given to them. Challenge them to use words that they learnt earlier in the unit to describe the texture of materials, such as *rough, smooth, soft* and *silky*, as well as new words, such as *stretchy* and *bumpy*.
c and d Check that learners can match the word to the texture of the fabric swatches for their 'fabric quilt'.

Further activities

- Ask learners to complete Workbook page 51: Glass.
- Display the Unit 4 digital resource slideshow, slide 6: Glass. Use it to review what learners know about the glass objects on the slide and where they have seen similar objects.

 Unit 4 slideshow, slide 6: Glass

Answers to slide 6:
a Things are made from glass so they can be transparent to let light through, and also so that people can see through the glass.
b Learners should link the items to things that they have seen at home, school, and so on.

- Create an area where learners can explore different fabrics. Place words linked to texture (such as *soft, smooth, bumpy, rough* and *silky*), as well as words such as *cold, warm, fluffy* and *furry*.
- Display the Unit 4 digital resource slideshow, slide 7: Fabrics. Ask learners different questions to find out what they know about fabrics, such as: *What do you think the things are made from? What do you think the fabrics feel like? Why do you think that fabric has been used? What is special about it?*

 Unit 4 slideshow, slide 7: Fabrics

Answers to slide 7:
a and b Encourage learners to use language such as *soft, silky, smooth, warm* and *fluffy*.

- Ask learners to make fabric pictures, such as of fish, birds, trees or flowers.
- Tie-dye pieces of fabric so that learners can find out how fabric is coloured. You could use natural dyes such as onion skins, pomegranate, beetroot, carrots or different kinds of berries.

Success criteria

While completing the activities, assess and record learners who can:
- use senses to explore and talk about glass and fabric
- talk about what glass and fabric are like
- recognise and name common materials
- sort fabrics into different groups
- use a grid to record different fabrics
- compare different fabrics.

 Workbook answers
Page 51 Glass
1 a True
  b False
  c True
  d False
2 Check learners' drawings.

What is fabric used for?

 Learner's Book
pages 88–89

 Workbook
page 52

Objectives

- Recognise and name common materials. (1Cp3)
- Sort objects into groups based on the properties of their materials. (1Cp4)
- Record stages in work. (1Eo3)
- Make comparisons. (1Eo4)
- Try to answer questions by collecting evidence through observation. (1Ep1)
- Decide what to do to try to answer a science question. (1Ep4)

Background information

The activities on page 88 of the Learner's Book further develop learners' knowledge of fabrics and properties of materials, such as *absorbency, stretchiness* and the ability to *keep something warm or cool* (insulating properties). Learners are asked how they could find out if a fabric is absorbent, stretchy or able to keep someone cool. Using talk partners, learners should share ideas of how to answer the question and then be allowed to try out their ideas using pieces of fabric. Some learners might suggest mopping up some water to find out if it soaks up the water (is absorbent). They could simply try to stretch fabric, and they can make simple comparisons, feeling fabric to see if it is cool or warm to touch. In doing this, they are deciding what to do to answer a question and collecting evidence through comparative observations to answer the questions.

The activities on page 89 of the Learner's Book introduce the names of different fabrics that they might be exposed to when exploring different fabrics. Try to ensure that fabrics such as wool, cotton and hessian are in the class fabric collection, as well as any other fabrics you can source. Make sure that learners are given the opportunity to sort these fabrics into groups.

Starter activity suggestions

- Introduce the word *absorbent* to learners. Ask them if they have heard it before and if they know what it means. Write the word for them on the board and get them to say the word. They could even sing the word, as well as break it down into the syllables (*ab-sorb-ent*). Tell the class that absorbent means to soak up water and other liquids. Ask them where they use fabrics for this, such as in the kitchen and bathroom. Ask them to make up an action for *absorbent*. For example, they could be pretending to mop something up. In this way, the class is supported in learning what this word means.

- Ask learners how they could find out if a fabric is absorbent. Get them to share ideas with others.

- Ask learners if they know what the word *stretchy* means. Give them some fabrics and ask them to decide how to find out if a fabric is stretchy or not. Get the class to say the word stretchy in a way that makes the word sound like what it means, for example: *strrrrrrrreeeeeeettttttttchhhhhhhhy.*

- Show learners pictures of people wearing clothes made from different fabrics. Ask some guiding questions to help them to identify that we wear clothes made from some fabrics to keep us warm, and clothes made from other fabrics to keep us cool. Ask learners to think about how they could find out which fabrics in their collections would keep them warm and which ones would be cool to wear. Let them share their ideas with others.

- Give learners samples of wool fabric, cotton fabric and hessian to explore and describe the textures. Ask learners to think about how they could find out if wool, cotton or hessian stretches, feels warm or cool, and if it is absorbent.

Activity notes and answers

Page 88 Activity 1

a Check how learners carry out a simple test to find out which of their fabrics are absorbent. Accept appropriate responses that show they understand what absorbent means, such as using each one to mop up a small puddle of water.

b Check how learners carry out a simple test to find out which of their fabrics are stretchy. Accept appropriate responses that show they understand what stretchy means, such as pulling the fabric.

c Check how learners carry out a simple test to find out which of their fabrics are cool or warm. Accept appropriate responses that show they understand how to answer the question, such as feeling the fabric with their hands, or wrapping it around their hand like a glove.

Different kinds of fabrics

 Activity notes and answers

Page 89 Activity 1

a and b Check that learners use appropriate fabrics and that they have chosen different fabrics for different items of clothing.

c Check that learners have labelled the fabrics glued onto their picture correctly.

Further activities

- Ask learners to complete Workbook page 52: Which material stretches the most?
- Extend learners' knowledge of different fabrics by giving them access to other fabrics, including velvet, lace, felt, corduroy, denim and silk. You could also include leather and discuss why it is not a fabric.
- Ask learners to design and make something, such as a bag, using an appropriate fabric.
- Give learners a selection of children's clothing and ask them to name the fabric(s) used.
- You could give learners card templates of people who do different jobs. Ask learners to make their clothing out of the most appropriate fabric and stick it on the template.
- Ask learners to make a fabric book and stick a label on with the name of the fabric, texture and property.

Assessment ideas

Assess if learners can choose different fabrics and which type of clothing they are used for. Put out either dolls or soft toys or card templates that say, for example: *Make a soft scarf for…*; *Choose a stretchy material to make a T-shirt for…*; and so on.

Success criteria

While completing the activities, assess and record learners who can:

- name materials that they are using
- sort materials into groups: absorbent, stretchy, keep someone warm or cool
- take photographs, create collage pictures and make fabric books
- compare materials
- find out how stretchy, absorbent or warm/cool fabrics are
- carry out a test to find out how stretchy, absorbent or warm/cool fabrics are.

 Workbook answers

Page 52 Which material stretches the most?

1 a 8 blocks

b wool

c 4 blocks

Is it waterproof?

 Learner's Book
pages 90–91

 Workbook
pages 53–54

 Digital Resource

Objectives

- Identify the characteristics of different materials. (1Cp2)
- Try to answer questions by collecting evidence through observation. (1Ep1)
- Make predictions. (1Ep3)
- Decide what to do to try to answer a science question. (1Ep4)
- Explore and observe in order to collect evidence (measurements and observations) to answer questions. (1Eo1)
- Record stages in work. (1Eo3)
- Compare what happened with predictions. (1Eo5)

Background information

The activities on pages 90 and 91 of the Learner's Book develop learners' knowledge of the property *waterproof*. Waterproof material is any material that is impervious to water; that is, it does not let water through. At this level, the idea is quite straightforward – learners test materials to find out if they are waterproof or not.

The main focus, therefore, is developing learners' scientific enquiry skills further, in particular making predictions, testing their predictions and then comparing what happened with their original predictions to see if they were correct. Learners should already know the word *predict*. This series of activities is an opportunity for them to complete the testing cycle from the question, through to predicting, carrying out a comparative test, looking at results and drawing simple conclusions so that they can answer the original question. As learners work, listen to their responses when asked to *predict*. Use this to assess whether the learners understand this scientific term, or whether they require additional support before moving on.

Starter activity suggestions

- Take learners outside so that they can take pieces of materials such as plastic, fabrics and paper, and pour water over them. They can use, for example, plastic water bottles or toy watering cans. Do remind them that 'scientists' are sensible when they work, so they should try very hard not to get wet.

- Learners will need experience of water on materials before they can predict. As they gain experience outdoors, use the word *predict* and remind them what it means. Give learners additional materials and ask them to place them in one of two hoops, labelled *waterproof* and *not waterproof*. The hoops could also be drawn with chalk on the playground.

- Tell learners that they are now going to test their materials to find out if they are waterproof and if their predictions were correct. You could provide each group with a table chalked large on the playground, so that learners can place the material and their result in the table. For example:

Material	Waterproof
[swatch of material]	☺
[swatch of material]	☹

- Once completed, ask learners to look carefully at the different materials, using both sight (using a hand lens) and touch. Ask them what they notice. For example, does one material have holes that might let the water through? Then it will not be waterproof.

 Activity notes and answers

Page 90 Activity 1

a and **b** You could support learners by preparing tables for them. You could also cut swatches the correct size for the table, so that they just have to choose and stick on. If necessary, show learners how to complete the table first so that they are sure what to do.

c Accept learners' predictions. They are going to test them, so at this stage they do not need to be correct. Listen and ask questions, so that you can access the reasoning behind their responses.

Testing our predictions

 Activity notes and answers

Page 91 Activity 1

a Listen to learners discussing their ideas. Encourage them to clarify their ideas by saying, *That's interesting, why have you decided to do that?* Also ask them to think forward, by asking, for example: *What do you think will happen if you do that?*

b Learners could place material swatches over a tray or container and pour water over them.

c Learners could use the jug, watering can or mug to pour water over the materials. They could do this over the tray to avoid getting water everywhere.

Page 91 Activity 2 The responses depend on the materials that the learners tested. They should be able to decide which were waterproof and share their ideas with others in the class, perhaps another pair. As they share, make sure that learners use the results in the table as proof of what happened.

Further activities

- Ask learners to complete Workbook page 53: Different fabrics and Workbook page 54: My clothes.

- Ask learners to complete the Unit 4 digital resource PCM1: Waterproof materials.

- Show learners the Unit 4 digital resource video clip: Waterproof. Talk about what is happening in the video and why it is important for the child's clothes and boots to be waterproof.

 Unit 4 PCM1: Waterproof materials

Answers to PCM1:
1 a hessian, silk, net   b Yes
  c Not waterproof
2 Drawings might show water being poured over swatches of the materials.

- Learners could wrap soft toys in different materials and pour water over to find out which material would keep the toys dry.

- Ask learners to explore the question *What other materials are waterproof?*

- Talk about other places where we use waterproof materials, such as houses, food wrapping and shoes.

 Unit 4 video clip: Waterproof

Success criteria

While completing the activities, assess and record learners who can:
- say which materials are waterproof
- observe their test to answer questions to find out which materials are waterproof
- predict which materials might be waterproof
- decide what to do to explain how they are going to test materials for being waterproof
- observe what happens and use observations to answer questions
- use a table to record their test
- compare the results of in their test with their predictions.

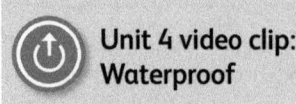 **Workbook answers**

Page 53 Different fabrics
1 a bag – hessian
  b T-shirt – cotton
  c jumper – wool
  d pair of socks – wool or cotton

Page 54 My clothes
1 Check learners' drawings and labels.
2 For example: raincoat, rain hat, Wellington boots, waterproof trousers.

Party problem

 Learner's Book
pages 92–94

 Workbook
pages 55–56

 Digital Resource

Objectives

- Identify the characteristics of different materials. (1Cp2)
- Try to answer questions by collecting evidence through observation. (1Ep1)
- Make predictions. (1Ep3)
- Decide what to do to try to answer a science question. (1Ep4)
- Explore and observe in order to collect evidence (measurements and observations) to answer questions. (1Eo1)
- Record stages in work. (1Eo3)
- Compare what happened with predictions. (1Eo5)

Background information

The activities on pages 92 and 93 of the Learner's Book support scientific enquiry skills, particularly testing learners' predictions through a simple comparative test. They will also experience making their own decisions and working independently to show what they can do. This provides an assessment opportunity.

Starter activity suggestions

- Give the class a party invitation for a class party based on 'using materials'. Ask learners what kind of things they will need for the party and what those things are made from, such as paper plates, plastic cups and spoons, ceramic serving plates and metal knives. Learners could also suggest different kinds of foods, referring back to the previous unit where they learnt about healthy foods.

- Tell learners that you will need to buy something to mop up spills, just in case anyone knocks over their drink. You could give a range of materials for learners to look at and predict which ones would be best, sorting the materials into 'will mop up' (absorbent) and 'will not mop up' (not absorbent). This can then lead them into a comparative test.

 ## Activity notes and answers

Page 92 Activity 1 Accept all responses, using this as an assessment of whether the learners recognise that plastic is waterproof and so will not be absorbent. If not, they will need some additional experience to distinguish between *absorbent* and *waterproof*.
Answer:
The plastic bag will not mop up water.

Page 92 Activity 2 Accept all responses and reasonings. Learners are going to test their predictions, so at this point there is no right answer.

Solving the party problem

 ## Activity notes and answers

Page 93 Talk partners
a Listen to the learners and their ideas. Ask why they are making their decisions to understand their reasoning.
b Accept their responses. It is important that they try out their own ideas. If they have problems, they should work to solve them, thereby developing their independence.
c Put out a range of resources for them so that they can make their own choices of what to use. This will develop their ability to make decisions and work independently.
d Before they begin, ask them to explain how they will know, for example: *Which of the fabrics will mop up the spill?* You might challenge them by asking what happens if they are all absorbent.

Page 93 Activity 1 Observe learners carrying out their comparative test. Did they keep to their original plan or change it? Could they solve any problems that occurred?

Page 93 Activity 2

a and b Check that learners' responses reflect their results. Some learners might still be at the stage where, regardless of the results, they say that their prediction was the best.

c Scaffold learners writing their answers – they could write it on a whiteboard and then copy it. Remind them to include an explanation of how they mopped up the spills.

What have you learnt about materials?

 Activity notes and answers

Page 94 Activity 1

Answers:

a Metal   b Plastic   c Wood   d Fabric

Page 94 Activity 2

Learners might draw, for example, a cushion, blanket, scarf or jumper. Ask them to talk about the object they have drawn and tell you how it feels.

Page 94 Activity 3

a Encourage learners to look around the classroom for plastic items if they need to. Write the labels for those learners who need support.

b Learners should now identify three things made from metal. Write the labels for learners who need support.

Further activities

- Ask learners to complete the digital resource interactive activity: Materials match-up. Challenge learners to match the objects with the correct materials.

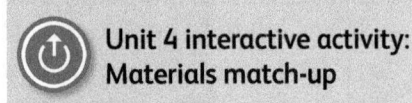 **Unit 4 interactive activity: Materials match-up**

- Ask learners to complete Workbook page 55: Mopping up spills, and Workbook page 56: On the way to school.

- Ask learners to complete the Unit 4 digital resource PCM2: Materials on the building site.

Unit 4 PCM2: Materials on the building site

Answers to PCM2:

1 a

- Have the party, and let learners take photographs of the party, including an 'accidental spill'. 'Accidentally' spill some juice on each table. Ask the learners to mop it up. Check what material(s) they choose. Did they use the 'result' from their test?

ICT links

Learners could use a computer party invitation template on which to write their sentence.

Assessment ideas

- The activities on pages 92 and 93 offer you the opportunity to observe learners and assess their ability to carry out a simple comparative test and answer their question.
- Ask learners to self-assess using the 'What can you remember?' checklist on page 94 of the Learner's Book, as well as the self-assessment table on page 57 of the Workbook.
- Ask learners to complete Quiz 2 on pages 95–96 in the Learner's Book. It provides an opportunity to revisit and assess key ideas from this unit.

Success criteria

While completing the activities, assess and record learners who can:

- say which materials are absorbent (will mop up spills)
- observe their test to answer questions about which materials are absorbent (will mop up spills)
- predict which material will be the best for mopping up spills
- decide what to do to try to answer how they are going to test materials
- observe what happens and use their observations to answer questions
- talk about or tell someone else how they did their test and what happened
- compare what happened with their predictions.

 **Workbook answers**

Page 55 Mopping up spills

1 a cloth

   b plastic bag

   c no

Page 56 On the way to school

1 Check learners' drawings and writing.

Quiz 2: Chemistry

Answers:

1 a – tree bark

2 Accept reasonable responses, such as pencil, chair, table, ruler.

3 A material that does not let water through is waterproof.

4 a – plastic football

5 a metal

  b wood

  c plastic

  d fabric

6 a The paper towel – it has three smiley faces.

  b The plastic bag – it has a frown face.

Unit 5 Forces

Objectives overview

Learning objective	Objective code	Learner's Book pages	Teacher's Pack pages	Workbook pages	Digital Resource Pack
Physics: Forces					
Explore, talk about and describe the movement of familiar things.	1Pf1	97, 98, 99, 100, 101, 102, 103, 104, 105, 106, 107, 108, 109, 110, 111, 112, 113, 114, 115	114, 115, 116, 117, 118, 119, 120, 121, 122, 123, 124, 125, 126, 127, 128, 129, 130, 131, 132	58, 59, 60, 61, 62, 63	Unit 5 slides 3, 4, 5, video clip 1
Recognise that both pushes and pulls are forces.	1Pf2	100, 101, 102, 103, 104, 105, 106, 107, 108, 109, 110, 111, 114, 115	116, 117, 118, 119, 120, 121, 122, 123, 124, 125, 126, 127, 128, 129, 130, 131, 132	59, 60, 61, 62, 63, 64, 65, 66	Unit 5 slides 3, 4, 5, 7, PCM2, video clip 1
Recognise that when things speed up, slow down or change direction there is a cause.	1Pf3	105, 106, 107, 108, 109, 110, 111, 112, 113, 114	122, 123, 124, 125, 126, 127, 128, 129, 130, 131, 132	61, 62, 63, 64, 65	Unit 5 video clip 2, PCM1
Scientific enquiry: Ideas and evidence					
Try to answer questions by collecting evidence through observation.	1Ep1	101, 104, 105, 106, 107, 108, 109, 110, 111	118, 119, 120, 121, 122, 123, 124, 125, 126, 127, 128, 129, 130	58, 59, 60, 61, 65	Unit 5 slide 5
Scientific enquiry: Plan investigative work					
Ask questions and contribute to discussions about how to seek answers.	1Ep2	105, 106, 107, 108	122, 123, 124, 125		Unit 5 slide 7

Learning objective	Objective code	Learner's Book pages	Teacher's Pack pages	Workbook pages	Digital Resource Pack
Make predictions.	1Ep3	102	118, 119	61	
Decide what to do to try to answer a science question.	1Ep4	109, 110	126, 127, 128	66	Unit 5 slide 5
Scientific enquiry: Obtain and present evidence					
Explore and observe in order to collect evidence (measurements and observations) to answer questions.	1Eo1	104	120, 121	62, 64, 65	Unit 5 slide 6, PCM2
Suggest ideas and follow instructions.	1Eo2			59, 63, 66	
Record stages in work.	1Eo3				
Scientific enquiry: Consider evidence and approach					
Make comparisons.	1Eo4	97, 98, 99, 100, 101	114, 115, 116, 117, 118, 119	58, 60	
Compare what happened with predictions.	1Eo5				
Model and communicate ideas in order to share, explain and develop them.	1Eo6	103, 104, 105, 106, 107, 108, 109, 110, 111, 112, 113	120, 121, 122, 123, 124, 125, 126, 127, 128, 129, 130		

How do things move?

Learner's Book
pages 97–98

Workbook
page 58

Objectives

- Explore, talk about and describe the movement of familiar things. (1Pf1)
- Make comparisons. (1Eo4)

Background information

The activities on pages 97 and 98 of the Learner's Book develop learners' knowledge about how things move. Movement is when something (including humans) changes location. Forces (pushes and pulls) make things speed up, slow down, change direction and stop.

Throughout this unit, focus on learners developing their confidence in using key words such as *move*, *movement*, *push*, *pull* and *force*. Take every opportunity to link this unit with physical education activities, both indoors and outdoors, as well as take the class on visits to places such as local parks, recreation grounds and sports facilities. It would also be useful to make a collection of toys that move, for learners to use throughout this unit.

These first pages provide an opportunity to elicit whether learners are familiar with basic vocabulary such as *move*, *walk*, *run*, *jog* and *crawl*, as well as *moving*, *walking*, *jumping*, and so on. As learners describe how they move, ask them to link these movements to the parts of the body being used. This will also provide an opportunity to reinforce and apply learning from Unit 2: Ourselves.

Starter activity suggestions

- Ask learners to think about, and share with a partner, which parts of their body they use to move.
- Ask learners to play 'Copy cat' and copy the movements their partner makes.
- Give learners a collection of pictures showing different ways in which people move. Ask them to sort them according to the movements, such as running or jumping.
- If possible, find a video clip from the internet showing the different ways in which animals move. Use this as a starting point for a discussion about how animals move.

 ### Activity notes and answers

Page 97 Activity 1
Answers:
The pictures show running, jumping and crawling.

Page 97 Activity 2
a and **b** Encourage them to think about, for example, games they play in school and at home.
c Learners write a sentence, such as: *I like to run fast.*

How do animals move?

 Activity notes and answers

Page 98 Talk partners Ask learners if they have ever seen any of the animals. You could ask them to move like, for example, a kangaroo or snake, encouraging them to use descriptive language.

Answers:

cheetah – running   snake – slithering   bird – flying

kangaroo – hopping   fish – swimming

Page 98 Activity 1

Answers:

- The cheetah is running.
- The snake is slithering.
- The bird is flying.
- The kangaroo is hopping.
- The fish is swimming.

Further activities

- Ask learners to complete Workbook page 58: How things move.
- Ask learners to mime different ways that animals move, and ask their partner to guess which animal they are.
- Ask learners to mime different ways that animals move to find food, shelter or to avoid being eaten.
- Ask learners to 'adopt' an animal and find out about it, in particular the way it moves when it feeds on plants or hunts other animals.
- Challenge learners to find out at home which is the fastest land animal, animal in the sea and animal in the air.

 ICT links

Learners could create a word file of topic words, or animal pictures with text to say how they move.

Success criteria

While completing the activities, assess and record learners who can:

- explore, talk about and describe how humans and some animals move
- make comparisons between things that move.

 Workbook answers

Page 58 How things move

1 ball – roll
  bird – fly
  child – run
  kangaroo – hop
  snake – slither
  baby – crawl
  fish – swim

Freeze frame

 Learner's Book
pages 99–100

 Workbook
page 59

 Digital Resource

Objectives

- Explore, talk about and describe the movement of familiar things. (1Pf1)
- Recognise that both pushes and pulls are forces. (1Pf2)
- Make comparisons. (1Eo4)

Background information

The activities on pages 99 and 100 introduce or build on learners' knowledge of specific vocabulary related to how things move. At this point, they are not expected to link this movement with forces (pushes and pulls), but to be able to link movement with the words to describe movements, such as *twist, turn, stretch* and *squash*.

This set of activities would be best carried out in a school hall or during a P.E. lesson where learners can explore and practise a range of movements, and describe what they are doing. As they work, challenge learners to link their movements to the parts of the body used. Reinforce basic language such as *turning around* and positional language such as *stretching high*. To support this, create extra-large word cards which can be displayed on the wall, or held up, for learners to read and then carry out the movement written on the card.

Support learners in understanding that when they move, they are causing the movement. They do not need something else to make them move, unlike a bat moving a ball, or someone pushing them.

Starter activity suggestions

- Ask learners to show you how they move their bodies to *twist, turn, stretch, spin, pull, push, kick* and *throw*. Make sure that all learners are able to do these movements. If any cannot, show them how, so that all learners understand these basic terms and their associated movements.
- Play the 'Copy cat' game again, where learners copy what you do and shout out the movement.
- Ask learners to put two movements together to make a short sequence, such as a twist and then a stretch.
- Challenge learners to make a sequence using all the types of movement on the word cards displayed on the wall. Give learners time to pair up with others and show them their sequences. As they do the sequences, other learners should shout out the name of each different movement they see.

 Activity notes and answers

Page 99 Talk partners
a Learners discuss the freeze-framed movement, of children stretching their arms above their heads.
b Observe learners copying the movement. Ask them which parts of the body they are using.
c Learners could take a photograph or make a short video clip.

Page 99 Activity 1
a Listen to learners reading the words, which could be placed on the hall wall so that they do not need to take their Learner's Books into the hall where they are doing the session.
b Observe learners miming each movement, to find out if they understand the movement.
c and d Partners freeze frame and take a photograph of each other. Support learners by modelling this approach with a pair to the rest of the class.

Actions

 Activity notes and answers

Page 100 Activity 1
Answers:
a stretching   b twisting   c squashing   d squeezing

Page 100 Activity 2 Observe learners miming these actions, to check that they know what the movement looks like. Ask learners to describe what they are doing. Ask them to name the movement and see if they can describe which movements use pushes and pulls. If some learners are unsure, give them objects to use so that they can carry out the movements.

Further activities

- Ask learners to complete Workbook page 59: Twisting, stretching and squashing.
- Ask learners to show each other their freeze frames from the Talk partners activity on Learner's Book page 99. They should describe the movement and body parts used.
- Ask learners to create a 'new' movement and give it a name, and then share it with the rest of the class. Other learners should say what they think about these movements: *It is interesting because ...*
- Challenge learners to create a sequence of movements to show the rest of the class. The other learners describe what they are doing.
- Create a collection of objects. Ask learners to find things which can stretch, twist, squash and squeeze.
- Display the Unit 5 digital resource slideshow, slide 3: How do they move? Ask learners to talk with their partner and describe how the living things shown on the slide are moving. Make sure that they use the language that they have been learning.

 Unit 5 slideshow, slide 3: How do they move?

Answers:
girl – walking; snake – slithering; boy – running/kicking; cheetah – running/sprinting; bird – flying/hovering; girl – throwing.

 ICT links

Ask learners to use cameras to take photographs and short video clips of themselves moving. Show learners how a video clip can be replayed to show slow motion. Ask learners to describe how they are moving their body.

Assessment ideas

Display the Unit 5 digital resource slideshow, slide 3: How do they move? It provides an assessment opportunity to make sure that learners know how different things move and can use the language that they have been learning. If there are any learners who have difficulty, ensure that they have additional experiences so that they are at the same stage as other learners in the class.

 Unit 5 slideshow, slide 3: How do they move?

Success criteria

While completing the activities, assess and record learners who can:

- explore, talk about and describe the movements squash, squeeze, twist, stretch, spin, turn
- say where a push or a pull is used to make something move
- make comparisons between the different movements.

 Workbook answers

Page 59 Twisting, stretching and squashing

1 a stretching

  b squashing

  c twisting

2 Check learners' drawings.

Pushes and pulls

Learner's Book
pages 101–102

Workbook
page 60

Objectives

- Explore, talk about and describe the movement of familiar things. (1Pf1)
- Recognise that both pushes and pulls are forces. (1Pf2)
- Make predictions. (1Ep3)
- Try to answer questions by collecting evidence through observation. (1Ep1)
- Make comparisons. (1Eo4)

Background information

The activities on pages 101 and 102 of the Learner's Book develop learners' knowledge that pushes and pulls are forces. Pushes and pulls (forces) can make things start moving or stop; they can also make things change direction. Get learners to act out pushes and pulls. As they do this, explain to them that when they push something, they are moving it away from themselves. When they pull something, they are moving the object closer to themselves. There is no need to say to learners 'push force' or 'pull force', because pushes and pulls are forces.

Ask learners to create actions to go with these words. They could, for example, suggest an action where they put their palms out in a pushing movement, then make two fists as if they are holding something and pull their fists towards themselves.

Practical hands-on experience is important. Some learners do find it difficult to differentiate between a push and a pull and to use the appropriate words. Provide many different opportunities to push and pull things, in addition to the activities on these pages. Use other areas in the school, including outdoors.

Learners should be clear in their understanding that *pushes* and *pulls* are *forces,* as this is key to the rest of this unit. It is important that you do not move on until the class understands these words and can demonstrate them to show their understanding.

Starter activity suggestions

- Get learners to act out a push and a pull: gently pushing their partner away from themselves and saying *push*, then gently pulling their partner towards them and saying *pull*.
- Show the class a video clip illustrating pushes and pulls in everyday life. While learners watch, ask them to call out and name any push or a pull that they see. Search on the internet for 'pushes and pulls' and/or 'everyday pushes and pulls'.
- Ask learners to discuss, with their talk partner or in a group, where they have seen pushes and pulls used around the classroom, school and home. Write their suggestions, and put them on the interactive whiteboard or on a working wall about forces.
- Give learners a collection of objects such as a calculator, a pen with a top, a ball, a box with a lid, a pencil case, a plastic bottle with a top, an eraser, a roll of kitchen paper, an elastic band, a clip, scissors and a glue stick. Ask them to decide if they should use a push or a pull (or a mixture of the two) when they use these objects.

Activity notes and answers

Page 101 Activity 1 Observe learners acting out a push or a pull, such as pushing a pram or pulling a chair. Make sure that if the learners are pushing and pulling each other, they do so sensibly.

Page 101 Activity 2

a, b and **c** Observe learners making things move by using a push or a pull. Listen to check that they can use the key words appropriately. Ask them to predict which force they will use and check their prediction.

d Learners draw what they did and then sort them into two sets: push and pull. The overlap section is for those objects that could be both pushed and pulled. You could give learners a copy of the Venn diagram on the photocopiable page: Pushes and pulls, on page 159 of this Teacher's Pack.

How do toys move?

 Activity notes and answers

Page 102 Talk partners

Learners discuss whether the toys in the pictures are moved by a push, a pull or both. Listen to partners talking to check that they are using pushes and pulls appropriately. Use this as a formative assessment point to help you make decisions about next steps.

Answers:

a balls – push

b horse – push and pull

c duck – pull

d bat and ball – push

e shopping trolley – push and pull

Further activities

- Ask learners to complete Workbook page 60: Pushes and pulls.

- If possible, learners could watch a video clip about forces being used in a playground, identifying pushes and pulls. Learners could use this approach in a local playground or in school, and show their clips to others in the class. Search on the internet by typing 'forces used in a playground'.

Success criteria

While completing the activities, assess and record learners who can:

- explore, talk about and describe how things move
- show that both pushes and pulls are forces
- predict whether they will need to use a push or a pull
- explore and observe pushes and pulls
- make comparisons between how things move.

 Workbook answers

Page 60 Pushes and pulls

1 a push
   b pull

2 door – push or pull
   swing – push or pull
   door bell – push
   shopping trolley – push or pull
   toy – pull

Making things move

 Learner's Book
pages 103–104

 Digital Resource

Objectives

- Explore, talk about and describe the movement of familiar things. (1Pf1)
- Recognise that both pushes and pulls are forces. (1Pf2)
- Try to answer questions by collecting evidence through observation. (1Ep1)
- Explore and observe in order to collect evidence (measurements and observations) to answer questions. (1Eo1)
- Model and communicate ideas in order to share, explain and develop them. (1Eo6)

Background information

The activities on page 103 of the Learner's Book reinforce the learning from previous pages on pushes and pulls. They also provide new contexts for learners to apply their knowledge and the language. The context of the photographs on Learner's Book page 103 is a playground and on page 104 is toys. You could also begin to discuss that the bigger the push or pull force, the bigger the movement. The key idea is that when something moves, there is always a force to make it move. For example, if a swing is not moving, a force is needed to make it move: a push or a pull. The same applies to other playground items. A seesaw will move downwards when a child sits on it; to move into the air, the child will need to push the ground with their feet. On a roundabout, someone will have to push or pull to make it move. The bigger the push or pull, the faster it will move. To stop the roundabout, a child could pull it or push against it to slow it down and make it stop.

On Learner's Book page 104 the aim is for learners to build on existing knowledge and understanding, and to combine this with recently introduced ideas, applying these ideas in a new activity where you can assess them to make sure that they are progressing.

Starter activity suggestions

- Display the Unit 5 digital resource slideshow, slide 4: Using forces, and slide 5: Making things move. Use the slides to revise how we can use pushes and pulls to make things move.

 Unit 5 slideshow, slide 4: Using forces, and slide 5: Making things move

Answers to slide 4:

Some learners will say words such as *press*. However, a press uses a push, so ask learners to think again about a press, letting them focus on the force words *push* or *pull*.

pushing down on calculator keys   pushing a ball
bird pulling a worm   squeezing a lemon (push)

Answers to slide 5:

pull the peach   push the ball   push or pull the train
push the table tennis ball   pull the toy duck

- Visit a local playground with the class, if possible. Explore the different rides and equipment, ensuring that learners do so safely. Make sure that they know to work scientifically, observing and thinking about how things move and what they have to do to make things move. Gather learners around specific playground equipment to demonstrate. Ask learners to think about and discuss the forces in action. Learners could video equipment in use and identify forces.

- If you are unable to visit a playground, search on the internet for a useful video clip. Do a search for: 'forces in the playground' or 'forces and playground equipment'.

- Collect a wide range of toys that move, including pull-along toys, for learners to explore. Let them find out how these toys move and which forces are needed.

Activity notes and answers

Page 103 Talk partners Listen to learners discussing each picture, to find out if they understand the forces being used.

Answers:

a To make the swing move, the girl standing needs to either push it or pull it, and then let go.

b The boy needs to use his legs to push himself upwards.

c The girl is using a push to make the roundabout move.

d To make herself move up the wall, the girl is pushing with her feet and using her arms to pull.

Make a pull-along toy

 Activity notes and answers

Page 104 Activity 1 Learners apply their knowledge of how things move and of design to make a pull-along toy. Provide them with either recyclable junk materials, such as boxes and string, or let them use construction materials. As they work, ask them to explain, using key scientific vocabulary, how they will make it move.

Page 104 Activity 2 Observe learners demonstrating their toy to others in the class. Listen to their explanations on how they make it move, and how they make it move faster, slower and change direction.

Further activities

● Ask learners to complete the Unit 5 digital resource PCM1: Look carefully.

 Unit 5 PCM1: Look carefully

Answers to PCM1:
1 a speeding up
  b stopped
  c a different direction
  d slowing down

● Show learners the Unit 5 digital resource video clip 1: Kneading dough. Ask them to watch carefully, think about, look out for and talk about the forces being used.

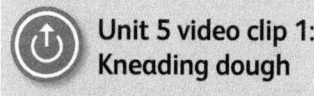 **Unit 5 video clip 1: Kneading dough**

 ICT links

Ask learners to make a video of playground equipment being used. They can create a voiceover which says which forces are being used to make things move.

Success criteria

While completing the activities, assess and record learners who can:

● explore, talk about and describe the movement of playground equipment and their pull-along toy

● recognise that both pushes and pulls are forces

● try to answer questions by observing playground equipment being used

● explore and observe in order to answer questions about how to make playground equipment and their pull-along toy move

● share their ideas and explain to other learners about forces in the playground and their pull-along toy.

Make them move

 Learner's Book
pages 105–106

 Workbook
page 61

Objectives

- Explore, talk about and describe the movement of familiar things. (1Pf1)
- Recognise that both pushes and pulls are forces. (1Pf2)
- Recognise that when things speed up, slow down or change direction there is a cause. (1Pf3)
- Try to answer questions by collecting evidence through observation. (1Ep1)
- Ask questions and contribute to discussions about how to seek answers. (1Ep2)
- Model and communicate ideas in order to share, explain and develop them. (1Eo6)

Background information

The activities on pages 105 and 106 of the Learner's Book challenge learners to apply what they already learnt about forces in different contexts. It is important that learners have frequent opportunities to apply their knowledge, understanding and skills in different contexts. This enables you and the learners to assess how secure their knowledge, understanding and skills are. On Learner's Book page 105, learners are given a problem to solve: they have to find a way to move cardboard box cars. To do so successfully, they need to have practical experience. They should make their own cardboard cars and sit in them, so that they can feel how difficult it is to move them.

On page 106, learners make their own set of skittles. Encourage independence by offering resources such as sand and pebbles, so that learners have to make a choice. As learners work, elicit their ideas and reasoning, as well as asking them to explain what forces are in action when they play the game.

Eliciting learners' ideas provides you with an opportunity to assess what learners already know and whether or not they require additional experiences to ensure that they are secure in their ideas before moving on. Discuss with learners how when the ball moves quickly, slows down and changes direction there is a reason, such as the way they threw the ball and also the direction in which they threw it.

Starter activity suggestions

- Provide learners with a range of toys that can be pushed and pulled. Ask the class to share ideas, describing how they work and the forces that are used to move them.
- Show learners a skittle game. Ask them to describe the forces that are used to play the game.
- Provide a range of resources for learners to explore. Ask them to discuss, with their partner or group, how they could use them to make their own skittles game.

Activity notes and answers

Page 105 Activity 1

a Give learners time to explore and discuss their ideas. You could also leave a range of resources around to prompt those discussions, such as rope, cut-down broom handles or thick wood rollers.
Give learners time to design their own car by using paints and recyclable objects such as plastic plates. Encourage learners to work together and discuss what they are going to do.

b Listen to the talk partners or small groups. When they are discussing how to make their car move, check whether the ideas are appropriate and use knowledge of pushes and pulls.

c Give learners time to make their car. Make sure that they focus on how to make the car move, using forces.

d Ask learners to predict what will happen when they test their car. When they have found out, ask them to reflect on whether their prediction was correct.

Page 105 Activity 2

a Learners could share what they have achieved with a pair or group in the class.

b As learners describe how they made their car work, ask them to compare what each other did and how it worked, using scientific language such as *push*, *pull* and *move*.

Skittles

 Activity notes and answers

Page 106 Activity 1

a Ask learners to work with a partner or in a small group to make their set of skittles.

b As learners play the skittles game, move around among the groups and ask them to describe what forces they are using on the ball: a push or a pull.

c Ask learners to describe what kind of force knocks the skittles over (a push or a pull) and whether it is a big or small force.

Further activities

- Create a big book about making and moving their cars and playing skittles games. Learners could take photographs for the book and write sentences or comments about the forces that are used.
- Have a class skittles competition.
- Allow learners to take their skittles game out at play and lunch time, so that other learners can play.

 ICT links

Ask learners to take photographs and create captions to make set of instructions for playing their skittles game. They should include what kind of forces to use and whether these forces should be big or small.

Success criteria

While completing the activities, assess and record learners who can:

- explore, talk about and describe how to move their car
- say when a force is being used to make something move, slow down and stop
- do something to show that pushes and pulls are forces
- be able to say what made something slow down, speed up or change direction
- ask questions about how to move the car, or how to make the skittles game and discuss how to answer their own questions
- show others what they have made and describe the forces used.

 Workbook answers

Page 61 Skittles

1 a rolls
  b pushes
  c pushes
  d bigger

Changing direction

 Learner's Book
pages 107–108

 Workbook
page 62

 Digital Resource

Objectives

- Explore, talk about and describe the movement of familiar things. (1Pf1)
- Recognise that both pushes and pulls are forces. (1Pf2)
- Recognise that when things speed up, slow down or change direction there is a cause. (1Pf3)
- Try to answer questions by collecting evidence through observation. (1Ep1)
- Ask questions and contribute to discussions about how to seek answers. (1Ep2)
- Model and communicate ideas in order to share, explain and develop them. (1Eo6)

Background information

The activities on pages 107 and 108 of the Learner's Book develop learners' knowledge of using forces to change the direction of a moving object. In science, it is important to elicit learners' understanding at the beginning of an activity. For example, ask learners what they think the word *direction* means. Their responses can provide you with an opportunity to assess if and what they know about this word. One useful way to collect learners' ideas is to write them onto a working wall or display, and then use their ideas to develop their understanding.

Using a cross-curricular approach can be a fun and appropriate way to start. For example, take the class into the school hall or out into the school grounds, along with P.E. equipment such as balls, bats and bean bags. Many activities in the forces unit could be carried out during a P.E. lesson. Learners can use their body and apparatus to show that things can move in different directions, such as *up*, *down*, *forwards*, *backwards*, and *sideways* to the *left* or to the *right*. It is important that learners have physical experiences to help them understand what these words mean to be able to use them with confidence.

Starter activity suggestions

- In the school hall or outdoors space, tell learners to run around and then shout, *Change direction!* Check that all learners recognise what to do.
- Give learners instructions on which direction to move in. Some learners might still be unsure of left and right, and could require support.
- Give learners directions for pushing (kicking a ball or hitting a ball with a bat). Each time, use the word *direction*, such as: *Change direction – push to the left, push forwards, push backwards.*
- Using pull-along toys from previous activities, learners could pull the toy and keep changing direction. They could work in pairs and tell their partner to change direction and which direction to go in.

 ### Activity notes and answers

Page 107 Talk partners
Answers:
a pull – B and D
b push – A, C and E

Page 107 Activity 1 Observe learners miming playing a game where they use a push or a pull to make something change direction. Ask learners to explain what they are doing, using the words *push*, *pull*, *move* and *change direction*.

Squirty forces

 Activity notes and answers

Page 108 Talk partners Listen to learners and support them in breaking down the action by asking what the girl does first, next, and so on. For example: She is squeezing the bottle and pushing the water out of the bottle. The water hits the skittle and pushes it over.

Page 108 Activity 1

a Encourage learners to draw on their experience of making the skittles game from page 106 of the Learner's Book.

b They will squirt water from a squirty bottle (empty washing-up liquid bottle or plastic bottle with a hole in the cap) at the bottles.

c Learners should be able to explain that they will have to move the water bottle so that the water squirts out in a different direction. Then it will push the skittles and they will fall in a different direction (the same direction as the push from the force of the water).

Page 108 Activity 2 Learners should apply what they know about using a push to move the ball, and also make it change direction so that it goes from one side of the playground to the other (in a straight line).

Page 108 Challenge yourself! Provide a range of different plastic bottles that learners could choose from and ask them to explain their choice, for example: *Was it size or the type of nozzle?*

Further activities

● Ask learners to complete Workbook page 62: Squirty bottle forces.

● Learners could play squirty water games with the skittles that they have made during playtime.

● Ask learners to complete the Unit 5 digital resource PCM2: Squirting water.

 Unit 5 PCM2: Squirting water

Answers to PCM2:
1 a water squirter   **b** 6 blocks   **c** paper fan   **d** water squirter

 ICT links

Ask learners to give 'teach- ins' to other classes to demonstrate their games, showing how forces are used to make something move and change direction. Ask learners to video their 'teach-in'. They can then watch the video and reflect on what they have learnt, such as using scientific vocabulary.

Success criteria

While completing the activities, assess and record learners who can:

● explore, talk about and describe how make something change direction

● show that pushes and pulls are forces

● be able to say what made something slow down, speed up or change direction

● use what they see to help answer their question

● ask questions about how to make their skittles game and discuss how to answer their own questions

● show others what they have made, describe the forces used and how to make a moving object change direction.

 Workbook answers

Page 62 Squirty bottle forces

1 a Anna
 b Josh
 c Peter
 d Anna
 e Peter

Blow football

Learner's Book pages 109–110

Workbook page 63

Digital Resource

Objectives

- Explore, talk about and describe the movement of familiar things. (1Pf1)
- Recognise that both pushes and pulls are forces. (1Pf2)
- Recognise that when things speed up, slow down or change direction there is a cause. (1Pf3)
- Try to answer questions by collecting evidence through observation. (1Ep1)
- Decide what to do to try to answer a science question. (1Ep4)
- Model and communicate ideas in order to share, explain and develop them. (1Eo6)

Background information

The activities on pages 109 and 110 of the Learner's Book support learners in working independently and applying their knowledge about forces.

On page 109, the activity lets learners explore how to move a table tennis ball. Focus learners' attention on cause and effect by asking: *What did you do that made the ball move?* Model language, such as the ball *speeds up*, *slows down* and *changes direction*. In this activity, you could focus learners' attention on the idea that a force can make the ball speed up and slow down, repeatedly modelling the words so that learners develop understanding in this context.

On page 110, learners ask their own questions and then discuss with their partner how they will find the answers. Support learners through effective questioning, for example: *What is your question? What do you think you could do to answer your own question? What do you think will happen? How can you record what you did and what happened?*

Encourage learners to make decisions and work independently. Challenge learners to think about how they could measure how far the ball goes. At this level, non-standard measurements such as feet, hand spans and blocks are fine. If some learners want to use a ruler or tape measure, help them to use and read the equipment.

Starter activity suggestions

- Give learners straws and table tennis balls. Allow time for them to explore and talk amongst themselves about how to make the ball move, change direction and speed without touching it.
- As a class, come to an agreement about what makes the table tennis ball move. The table tennis ball is light; the learners blow air (from their lungs) into the straw; it comes out at the other end; then the air touches the ball and the force of the moving air makes the ball move.
- Ask learners to explain to each other, and help each other to understand what it is happening. They should be able to talk to each other as they work, explaining what is happening and consolidating the ideas.

Activity notes and answers

Page 109 Activity 1

c Learners should be able to describe that it is the air from their lungs or mouth that is going into and out of the straw, that is pushing the table tennis balls, as well as various factors that affect why some balls travel further (such as that they blew harder on one of them, that one ball was closer or further away, and so on).

Page 109 Talk partners
Example answers:

a *I blew hard in the straw, and the bigger force of the air pushed the ball a long way (distance).*
b *I blew softly, and the smaller force of the air pushed the ball only a little way (distance).*
c *I blew hard, the air pushed the ball and it moved faster.*
d *I blew from a different direction, such as from the side, and it made the ball change direction.*

Page 109 Activity 2 You could ask learners to write a sentence to add to their picture to say what they did to make the ball move. Write them for those learners who may need help.

What is your question?

 Activity notes and answers

Page 110 Talk partners Write them for those learners who need support with writing.

Page 110 Activity 1

a The practical activity will depend on the questions learners have asked.

b If a camera is available, learners could take photographs of themselves carrying out their activity.

c Learners could use the photographs to help them explain what they did. Listen closely to make sure they are using correct scientific language.

Further activities

- Ask learners to complete Workbook page 63: Pushing and pulling and Workbook page 64: Paper ball race.
- Display the Unit 5 digital resource slideshow, slide 6: Moving a table tennis ball. Ask the class to use the data on the bar graph to answer the questions on the slide.
- Ask learners to find out if they can move balls made of different materials such as kitchen foil, tissue, card and newspaper. How could they measure how far each one went? Support learners in recording this activity, the results could then be converted into a pictogram.

 Unit 5 slideshow, slide 6: Moving a table tennis ball

Answers to slide 6:

a The children could have blown the table tennis ball and measured how far it went, using blocks.

b Ana

c 8 blocks

Assessment ideas

The activities on pages 109 and 110 provide an opportunity to observe and assess learners to find who are able to ask their own questions, stay on task and complete the activities. You can assess who are able to talk to others about what they have done and found out, using key vocabulary such as *forces, push, move, change direction, prediction, happened*.

Success criteria

While completing the activities, assess and record learners who can:

- explore, talk about and describe the movement of familiar things
- recognise that both pushes and pulls are forces
- say what they have to do to make the table tennis ball speed up, slow down or change direction
- answer their own question through observing what happens
- decide what to do to try to answer their science question
- show someone else and describe how a blow football game works, using science words.

Workbook answers

Page 63 Pushing and pulling

1 a pulling

   b For example: *She will have to pull the kite in a different direction, up or down, left or right.*

   c pushing

   d For example: *He will have to push the ball in a different direction, up or down, left or right.*

   e pulling

   f For example: *They will have to pull the rope in a different direction: up or down, left or right.*

Page 64 Paper ball race

1 a battery fan　　　b newspaper　　　c 10 bricks

   d The battery fan, because it pushed the ball the furthest.

Bubbles

 Learner's Book
pages 111–113

 Workbook
page 65

 Digital Resource

Objectives

- Explore, talk about and describe the movement of familiar things. (1Pf1)
- Recognise that both pushes and pulls are forces. (1Pf2)
- Recognise that when things speed up, slow down or change direction there is a cause. (1Pf3)
- Try to answer questions by collecting evidence through observation. (1Ep1)
- Model and communicate ideas in order to share, explain and develop them. (1Eo6)

Background information

The activity on page 111 of the Learner's Book provide an opportunity for learners to apply what they know about making things move, using the context of bubbles. This is an assessment opportunity, where you can find out which learners are able to apply knowledge and talk with confidence about forces, using appropriate language. Bubbles are an engaging context which will challenge learners to apply what they know. The key understanding is that they force (push) air into the bubble wand, which then makes a bubble. The harder they blow, the more air they force (push) into the bubble, which pushes the mixture to make a larger bubble. If they force (push) too much air into the bubble, it will burst. The force of the air moving (wind) then pushes the bubbles around.

The activities on pages 112 and 113 of the Learner's Book provide another context for learners to explore and apply what they know about forces. The aims of this section on kites are for learners to know that wind is moving air, and that moving air makes some things move, such as a kite. This is an activity where you should encourage independence, so that the kite learners make is their own, and not produced by the adult.

Starter activity suggestions

- Take learners out into the school grounds to blow bubbles, using a range of bubble wands.
- Ask learners to work out with a partner how they make a bubble, using forces.
- Ask learners to work out with a partner what makes the bubbles move once they have been made.
- Show learners the Unit 5 digital resource video clip 2: Flying a kite. Talk about how the boy is flying the kite. *What is he doing to the string?*
- Bring into the classroom different kites for learners to look at, such as kites made using dowelling and paper or plastic bags. Ask learners to think about how they could use some of the ideas to make their own kite.

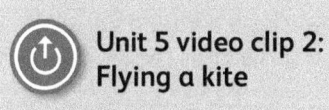 Unit 5 video clip 2: Flying a kite

Activity notes and answers

Page 111 Activity 1
Answers:
a Do not force (push) too much air into the bubble.
b Push lots of air into the bubble.
c The bubble is smaller or gets bigger more slowly.
d The bubble gets bigger quickly and it might burst.
e Move the bubble-maker up, down or sideways and blow bubbles; wave the bubble wand around instead of blowing into it.

Page 111 Challenge yourself!

a Learners could suggest that they have to blow harder. If so, encourage them to think about the direction. If they need the bubble to go up, they should blow upwards.

b The bubble might burst or no bubble is formed.

Make a kite 1 and Make a kite 2

 Activity notes and answers

Pages 112 and 113 Activity 1 Before learners begin to make their kite, ask them to look at the pictures and read through the instructions with them. Ask them to work with partners and decide if there is any part of the instructions that they do not understand. Encourage independence and collaboration. Even if they make one kite each, they should help each other with 'fiddly' parts.

Further activities

- Ask learners to complete Workbook page 65: Playing with bubbles.

- If possible, find a video on the internet that shows bubbles forming in slow motion. Show the learners and ask them to explain how bubbles are made using key forces vocabulary.

- Watch a video clip showing kites flying, such as one showing an international kite festival in China. Discuss the kites: *Why do they need lots of wind to fly? How do people make them move in different directions? What forces are used?*

- Have your own kite flying festival where learners fly their kites in the school grounds during playtime, so that other classes or the rest of the school can watch.

Success criteria

While completing the activities, assess and record learners who can:

- explore, talk about and describe the movement of bubbles and kites

- recognise that both pushes and pulls are forces

- say what they have to do to make bubbles move and change direction

- answer their own question through observing what happens

- show someone else and describe how bubbles are made and how kites move, using science words.

 Workbook answers

Page 65 Playing with bubbles

1 a blow
  b harder; force
  c pushes
  d direction

Fly your kite

 Learner's Book
pages 114–115

 Workbook
page 66

 Digital Resource

Objectives

- Explore, talk about and describe the movement of familiar things. (1Pf1)
- Recognise that both pushes and pulls are forces. (1Pf2)
- Recognise that when things speed up, slow down or change direction there is a cause. (1Pf3)

Background information

The activities on page 114 of the Learner's Book consolidate learning about forces and apply the ideas in the context of kites, which will offer an opportunity for the teacher to assess whether learners have mastered the ideas , for example, asking learners how they can make their kite speed up and slow down, and if the wind makes the kite speed up and slow down.

The activities on page 115 of the Learner's Book provide additional activities where learners can share what they know about forces at the end of this unit. Use these with Workbook page 66: How I use forces, and the Unit 5 digital resource slideshow, slide 7: Force of water. These will engage learners in activities that provide you with additional opportunities to ensure that learners have mastered the ideas in this unit, and are secure in their understanding.

 Unit 5 slideshow, slide 7: Force of water

Starter activity suggestions

- Take the whole class outside and give them time to learn how to fly their kites. Make sure that learners work carefully and do not trip and fall.
- As learners discover how to fly their kites, they can then begin to change what the kite does, such as change direction and fly at different heights.
- Stop the class and ask a child to demonstrate. The others watch and then talk with a partner, describing what forces are used to make the kite fly.
- Ask learners to think about this: *If you are pulling the kite, what is pushing it (wind/moving air)?*

Activity notes and answers

Page 114 Activity 1 As learners fly their kites, walk around among them, asking them to explain what they have to do to make the kite change direction or move towards them, and the effect of pulling the string.

Example answers:
a Pull the string in a different way, such as down, sideways or upwards.
b Pull the string downwards, in their direction or towards them.
c The kite is pulled in the same direction as the pulling action.

Page 114 Activity 2 Ask learners to write a sentence that includes the following: pulling the kite in their direction, pulling the kite so it changes direction, and any other explanation relating to the movement of the kite.

Page 114 Activity 3:

Example answers:
a How did you make it fly well? Did you let more string out?
b You run with the kite and let it go into the air. The air pushes the kite.
c Shape, colour, it can fly high, it can loop the loop.
d You could put streamers on it for a tail to make it look interesting when it flies, or make it bigger so that more air can push it.

What have you learnt about forces?

 Activity notes and answers

Page 115 Activity 1
Answer:
The bird is pulling the worm.

Page 115 Activity 2
Answers:
a jumping   **b** flying   **c** slithering   **d** sliding

Further activities

- Ask learners to complete Workbook page 66: How I use forces.
- Display the Unit 5 digital resource slideshow, slide 7: Force of water. Use it to assess whether learners can apply their knowledge and use scientific vocabulary to describe how the force of the water from the water squirter can make something move and change direction.

 Unit 5 slideshow, slide 7: Force of water

Answers to slide 7:
a For example, you push the squirter; the squirter pushes the water out and the water pushes things over; the water can make things move and change direction.
b Listen to learners discussing their ideas.

- Ask learners to think about their favourite activity in this unit, saying why they liked it and what they learnt. Tell them to work in pairs. They can look through the unit pages and share ideas.
- Collect what learners say they know about forces and add them to your working wall or display on forces.
- Learners could make another kite at home with their family. They can then bring it to school to show the class, while describing how to make it work by using forces vocabulary.
- Have a kite flying celebration/festival at a time when other classes can observe.

Success criteria

While completing the activities, assess and record learners who can:
- explore, talk about and describe the movement their kites
- say that they pull the strings of the kite and the wind pushes the kite
- describe how to speed up their kite, slow it down and change the direction by pulling on the kite string.

 Workbook answers

Page 66 How I use forces
1 Check learners' drawings and sentences.

Assessment ideas

Ask learners to self-assess using the 'What can you remember?' checklist on page 115 of the Learner's Book, as well as the self-assessment table on page 67 of the Workbook.

Unit 6 Sound

Objectives overview

Learning objective	Objective code	Learner's Book pages	Teacher's Pack pages	Workbook pages	Digital Resource Pack
Physics: Sound					
Identify many sources of sound.	1Ps1	116, 117, 118, 119, 120, 121, 123, 125, 126, 127, 128, 129, 130, 131, 132, 133, 134, 135, 136	135, 136, 137, 138, 139, 140, 141, 142, 143, 144, 145, 146, 147, 148, 149, 150, 151, 152, 153, 154	68, 69, 70, 71, 72, 73, 75, 76, 77, 78, 79	Unit 6 slides 3, 4, PCM1
Know that we hear when sound enters our ear.	1Ps2	116, 117, 118, 119, 120, 121, 122, 123, 124, 125, 126, 127, 128, 129, 130, 131, 135, 136	135, 136, 137, 138, 139, 140, 141, 142, 143, 144, 145, 146, 147, 148, 149, 150, 153, 154	68, 69. 70, 71, 72, 73, 74, 75, 76, 77, 78, 79	Unit 6 slides 3, 4, 5, video clips 1, 2, PCM2
Recognise that as sound travels from a source it becomes fainter.	1Ps3	128, 129, 130, 131, 132, 133	147, 148, 149, 150, 151, 152	76, 77	Unit 6 slides 6, 7
Scientific enquiry: Ideas and evidence					
Try to answer questions by collecting evidence through observation.	1Ep1	116, 117, 118, 119, 120, 121, 122, 123, 126, 127	135, 136, 137, 138, 139, 140, 141, 142, 145, 146	68, 69, 72, 76	
Scientific enquiry: Plan investigative work					
Ask questions and contribute to discussions about how to seek answers.	1Ep2				Unit 6 slide 6
Make predictions.	1Ep3	121, 132	139, 140, 151, 152	73	
Decide what to do to try to answer a science question.	1Ep4	126, 130, 131, 132	145, 146, 149, 150, 151, 152	70, 72	

Learning objective	Objective code	Learner's Book pages	Teacher's Pack pages	Workbook pages	Digital Resource Pack
Scientific enquiry: Obtain and present evidence					
Explore and observe in order to collect evidence (measurements and observations) to answer questions.	1Eo1	118, 119, 120, 121, 123, 128, 130, 131, 132, 133	137, 138, 139, 140, 141,142 147, 148, 149, 150, 151, 152	77	Unit 6 slide 7
Suggest ideas and follow instructions.	1Eo2	120, 121, 126, 128	139, 140, 145, 146, 147, 148	72, 74, 78, 79	
Record stages in work.	1Eo3	126, 127	145, 146		
Scientific enquiry: Consider evidence and approach					
Make comparisons.	1Eo4	116, 117, 118, 119, 122, 123, 128, 129, 130, 131	135, 136, 137, 138, 141, 142, 147, 148, 149, 150	68, 72	PCM2
Compare what happened with predictions.	1Eo5	132	151, 152	75	
Model and communicate ideas in order to share, explain and develop them.	1Eo6	133	151, 152	75	

Ears are for hearing

 Learner's Book
pages 116–117

 Workbook
pages 68–69

 Digital Resource

Objectives

- Identify many sources of sound. (1Ps1)
- Know that we hear when sound enters our ear. (1Ps2)
- Try to answer questions by collecting evidence through observation. (1Ep1)
- Make comparisons. (1Eo4)

Background information

The activities on pages 116 and 117 of the Learner's Book develop learners' understanding that hearing is one of the five senses. We hear sounds around us through sound entering our ears. At this stage, learners do not need to know the internal workings of the ear or that sounds are made by something vibrating. These aspects are dealt with in later stages.

The aims of the activities are for learners to explore a wide range of sounds and to understand that things that make a sound are called sources of sound. Collect a wide range of sound makers, including musical instruments, prior to starting this unit, so that learners have a wide range of objects to explore.

In the 'Further activities' section, learners copy a simple test shown on a video clip. This provides an excellent opportunity to use and develop scientific enquiry skills.

You could begin the unit by eliciting learners' ideas to provide you with an opportunity to assess what learners already know. The first set of starter activities is designed to support this.

Starter activity suggestions

- Provide groups of learners with a range of objects that make and do not make sound. This is a noisy activity, so it could be done outside the classroom in the school grounds. Ask learners to find out which objects make a sound and which do not, which sounds they like and which they do not, what kind of sound it is, and whether the sound is loud or quiet. Visit groups and listen to their discussions. Ask questions, using terms such as *sound*, *ears* and *source of sound* to test their knowledge.

- Challenge learners to be quiet for 30 seconds to one minute. They could put their heads on their arms on their desks, close their eyes and listen for sounds. At the end of the time, ask which sounds they heard and what they think the source of each sound was. This can be repeated outside, with learners sitting with their eyes closed.

 Activity notes and answers

Page 116 Talk partners

a Listen to learners sharing ideas. Accept appropriate answers which could be based on their own experiences, such as someone reading a funny story.

b Yes.

c Most learners will recognise facial expressions and body cues, such as children smiling and laughing, and hands on faces in surprise.

Page 116 Activity 1

a and b Ask learners to share their thoughts with a partner. Responses will be personal to the individual.

c Check the table that the learners complete. Some might use pictures. Those learners who have writing skills could add words.

You could give learners the photocopiable page: Sources of sound, on page 160 of this Teacher's Pack, to support this activity.

Answers:

children, trumpet, sitar, bird, plane, cat, car

Sounds all around you

 Activity notes and answers

Page 117 Activity 1
Answers: **a** bird   **b** cat   **c** drum   **d** girl   **e** bee   **f** thunder

Further activities

- Ask learners to complete Workbook page 68: Sounds that I do not like, and Workbook page 69: Sources of sound.

 Unit 6 slideshow, slide 3: The senses

Answers to slide 3:
a Sight, hearing, touch, taste, smell
b and **c** Learners compare what they have heard while being quiet with a partner.

- Display the Unit 6 digital resource slideshow, slide 3: The senses. Use it to check that learners know the five senses.
- Display the Unit 6 digital resource slideshow, slide 4: Sources of sound. Use it to check that learners know what a sound source is and can say what sound each one is making.

 Unit 6 slideshow, slide 4: Sources of sound

Example answers to slide 4:
a thunder – booms   **b** aeroplane – roars   **c** bird – cheeps
d baby – gurgles   **e** drum – bangs

- Ask learners to bring sources of sound from home (with permission), either objects or pictures, to make a class collection.

 ICT links

Learners could go around inside the school or outside in the school grounds to record sounds. They then play them back for the rest of the class to guess what the sound is, as well as the source of the sound.

Success criteria

While completing the activities, assess and record learners who can:
- identify many sources of sound
- say that we hear when sound enters our ear
- answer questions about sources of sound by listening
- make comparisons between different sounds.

 Workbook answers

Page 68 Sounds that I do not like
Check learners' drawings and sentences.

Page 69 Sources of sound
1 bee – buzz
  lion – roar
  clock – tick tock
  cat – meow
  firework – bang
2 Check learners' drawings and sentences.

Musical sounds

Learner's Book
pages 118–119

Workbook
page 70

Objectives

- Identify many sources of sound. (1Ps1)
- Know that we hear when sound enters our ear. (1Ps2)
- Try to answer questions by collecting evidence through observation. (1Ep1)
- Explore and observe in order to collect evidence (measurements and observations) to answer questions. (1Eo1)
- Make comparisons. (1Eo4)

Background information

The activities on pages 118 and 119 of the Learner's Book extend learners' experience of sound makers. As you work with learners, model the key language associated with this unit, such as *sources of sound*, *sound*, *ears* and *hearing*. Model scientific vocabulary by asking the class: *What do you think the source of the sound is?* rather than asking what the sound is, which will elicit an answer describing the sound itself.

The focus of the activities on Learner's Book page 118 is to provide learners with experiences of making sounds by using musical instruments. Here the aim is for learners to identify what they do to make the instrument make a sound.

On Learner's Book page 119, learners explore different materials to find out how they can be made to make a sound. Then they make their own sound board by using those materials. Make sure that learners have access to a wide range of everyday materials. Before they make their board, let them explore the materials and compare the sounds that they make.

Starter activity suggestions

- Revise previous learning about sound, sources of sound and that we hear with our ears. Play a recording of sounds. Ask learners to say what the source of each sound is and how they hear it.
- Revise previous learning about sources of sound by playing a game with the class. Let one learner come to the front of the class. Without the others seeing, this learner picks a sound maker from a box and makes a sound with it. The class has to work out what the source of the sound is.
- Revise previous learning by using a video clip of sounds from the internet. Ask learners to close their eyes and listen to the sounds, thinking about what is making the sound (the source of the sound). Then show the video clip again so that learners can see if they have named the sources of sound correctly.
- Engage learners in an activity where they compare different sounds, such as using the class collection of sound makers, describing how they are similar and different.

Activity notes and answers

Page 118 Activity 1

a As learners explore the different musical instruments, make sure that they know that these are sources of sound.

b As they explore the different musical instruments, observe how they make the sound. Let them name what they are doing by choosing from the words *bang*, *pluck*, *blow*, *tap*, *scrape* and *shake*. Before or during the activity, you may need to ask learners to demonstrate these words to check that they know what they mean, and how they are used to make instruments make a sound.

Page 118 Activity 2

a Some learners could take photographs showing themselves making sounds.

b Ask learners to write a sentence describing how their musical instrument makes a sound. Write them for those who need support.

Page 118 Challenge yourself! For example, learners could shake or tap a tambourine.

Make a sound board

 Activity notes and answers

Page 119 Talk partners Listen to talk partners to find out if they are able to work out how the sound board is made, in preparation for making their own. You could leave a set of resources out for them as prompts. Encourage them to try out different materials, as well as to compare the sounds that the sound boards make to help them make choices.

Page 119 Activity 1

a Learners make their own sound board, using different materials to make a range of sounds. Before starting this activity, make sure that they understand that the purpose of the sound board is to make different sounds when they hit it or roll a pencil over it. Materials could include corrugated card, glass paper (sand paper) and aluminium foil.

b Give learners time to share their boards with others in the class and explain how they were made. Listen to their discussions to find out if they understand what the source of the sound is.

c Listen to learners comparing the sounds and discussing which material makes the loudest sound.

d Listen to learners comparing sounds and discussing which material they think makes the most interesting sound. Encourage learners to explain why.

Further activities

- Ask learners to complete Workbook page 70: Making sounds.
- Some learners might take music lessons and be proficient in playing a musical instrument. If so, they could show learners how they play their instrument, explaining how sounds are made. It is a good opportunity to explain to learners that science is useful for many things, such as playing an instrument. It also celebrates the talents of individuals in the class.
- Ask the school music teacher, or someone else in the school with musical ability, to perform in front of the class. Allow the learners to explore how different musical instruments make sound.
- Let learners listen to, and compare, different kinds of music, such as drumming, guitars or brass bands. Discuss which music the class likes or dislikes, and how the instruments make the sound. Show pictures of the different sources of sounds (instruments).
- Encourage learners to make their own instruments at home and bring them to school to share with the class. Ask them to explain how they make the sound.

 ICT links

Learners could take photographs of their sound board being used or make a video. They can then use it to explain how it was made and the sounds it makes.

Success criteria

While completing the activities, assess and record learners who can:

- identify different sources of sound, such as musical instruments
- know that we hear when sound enters our ear
- answer their own questions (such as which materials they will use for their sound board) by observing (listening) to the sounds made
- explore and listen to the sounds of different materials and instruments to answer questions
- make comparisons between different sounds.

 Workbook answers

Page 70 Making sounds

1 a triangle – hit
  b maracas – shake
  c trumpet – blow
  d sitar – pluck
  e drum – hit

What can you hear?

 Learner's Book
pages 120–121

 Workbook
pages 71–72

 Digital Resource

Objectives

- Identify many sources of sound. (1Ps1)
- Know that we hear when sound enters our ear. (1Ps2)
- Try to answer questions by collecting evidence through observation. (1Ep1)
- Make predictions. (1Ep3)
- Explore and observe in order to collect evidence (measurements and observations) to answer questions. (1Eo1)
- Suggest ideas and follow instructions. (1Eo2)

Background information

The activities on pages 120 and 121 of the Learner's Book develop learners' understanding of the sense of hearing – that sounds are heard when they enter the ears in humans and other animals. There is also a focus on learners working scientifically and independently to make their animal ears from pictures. Learners may find this easier if they discuss their ideas in pairs, which might lead to them rethinking and changing ideas.

On Learner's Book page 120, learners make a headband with a large pair of ears to wear. Interestingly, these do make a difference. It encourages them to listen more carefully to sounds.

On Learner's Book page 121, learners make sound tins or boxes. These can be small cardboard boxes, plastic containers or metal tins with lids. Learners use a range of small objects made from different materials that they can put in their containers to make different sounds when they shake the containers. You might need to support some learners in using the words quiet and loud. Encourage them to apply prior knowledge of materials to think about the objects making the sound.

Starter activity suggestions

- Tell learners that they are going to put their hands over their ears. Ask them to predict what will happen and then try it to see if they were correct. Then make a noise, such as striking a triangle or shaking maracas. Ask learners to identify the source of the sound. They must then put their hands over their ears and describe what happens when the same sounds are repeated.

- Repeat the activity, this time asking learners to compare similarities and differences between placing their hand over their right ear and then their left ear.

- Ask the class to talk in groups about why two ears are better than only one ear. Collect their ideas.

 Activity notes and answers

Page 120 Activity 1

a Encourage learners to work in pairs to help each other. If appropriate, make a headband as well, so that they can see how it is constructed. You might need to support learners in working out how to make the headband the correct size for their head, such as using string to measure it.

b–d Learners can record the sounds they hear, using words and/or pictures.

Page 120 Challenge yourself! If learners use their 'big ears' at home, ask them to bring a list or photographs of the sources of sound they heard to share with the class. Were they similar or different to those they heard at school?

Mystery sounds

 Activity notes and answers

Page 121 Activity 1

a Support learners in thinking about putting objects made from different materials into each container. Encourage them to think about what kind of sound each one will make.

b Make sure that learners have not shown their partner what is inside their containers. Tell them they need to keep it a secret, because their partner has to predict what is inside.

c Encourage learners to listen carefully, to be quiet and think about the sound they hear, instead of saying the first thing they think of. This will develop their listening skills.

Page 121 Challenge yourself!

Encourage learners to make the sounds more challenging, for example, quieter, or more unusual so that their partner has to listen carefully, concentrate and think about what kind of material the object might be made from that could make that sound.

Further activities

- Ask learners to complete Workbook page 71: Amazing sounds, and Workbook page 72: Sound boxes.
- Display the Unit 6 digital resource slideshow, slide 5: Using ears to hear. Use it to find out what learners understand about hearing and how using one or two ears affects what can be heard.

 Unit 6 slideshow, slide 5: Using ears to hear

Answers to slide 5:

a Learners should notice that they hear less with only one ear, and mainly hear from one direction.

b Learners should notice that with two ears, they hear more and from different directions.

c Accept ideas such as so that they can hear more, and hear from different directions.

- Ask learners to complete the Unit 6 digital resource PCM1: Match the sound.

 Unit 6 PCM1: Match the sound

Answers to PCM1:

rain – pitter-patter; snake – hiss; drum – bang; doorbell – ring; baby – gurgle; lion – roar; owl – hoot

- Talk about people who are hearing-impaired and how some need to wear a hearing aid. The hearing aid makes some sounds louder, so that the person is able to hear better.

Assessment ideas

Use the learners' 'big ears' headbands to find out if learners understand that we hear with our ears, that we hear things that make sounds, and that these things are called sources of sound.

Success criteria

While completing the activities, assess and record learners who can:

- identify many sources of sound
- know that we hear when sound enters our ear
- try to answer questions through listening
- predict which object makes the sound in each container
- explore and observe (listen) to answer questions about using their 'big ears'
- suggest ideas and follow instructions.

 Workbook answers

Page 71 Amazing sounds

1 Check learners' writing.

Page 72 Sound boxes

1 Quiet: feather, fabric, paper.
Loud: stone, plastic cube, button.

2 Accept all reasonable answers, such as coins, card, beads.

Animal ears

 Learner's Book
pages 122–123

 Workbook
page 73

 Digital Resource

Objectives

- Identify many sources of sound. (1Ps1)
- Know that we hear when sound enters our ear. (1Ps2)
- Try to answer questions by collecting evidence through observation. (1Ep1)
- Explore and observe in order to collect evidence (measurements and observations) to answer questions. (1Eo1)
- Make comparisons. (1Eo4)
- Suggest ideas and follow instructions. (1Eo2)

Background information

The activity on page 122 reinforces the idea that animals have ears to help them hear. Not all animal ears are the same shape or size. Different animals have different ears because they have adapted to their environment. Like humans, animal ears are designed to collect sounds. Animals that are predators (eat other animals) usually have ears that face forward, so that they can focus on listening for their prey. Animals that are prey (eaten by other animals) often have ears that can move around. This helps them to listen for sounds from different directions, so that they can hear a predator creeping up on them.

The activities on page 123 focus on the idea that some sounds are so loud that they can hurt and damage our ears. Some people therefore need to wear earmuffs (ear defenders) to block the sound and protect their ears. Make sure that learners know that listening to very loud sounds can be dangerous for their ears. For example, if they are listening to music and they can 'feel' the music or it begins to hurt, it is too loud and could damage their hearing. If they are listening to music through earbuds or headphones and someone else can hear the sound, it is too loud. Over time, exposure to such loud music can damage hearing.

Starter activity suggestions

- If possible, show a video clip that has clips of human and animal ears. Do an internet search for: 'sound and hearing'. Ask learners to think about what they watched. Were all ears the same size and shape and in the same place?
- Ask learners to sit while their partner draws their ear. Explain that it is very hard to draw your own ear, as you cannot see it properly.
- Put out a collection of earmuffs and defenders for learners to wear to experience how they work and muffle and block sound. Allow pairs to go outside into the school grounds to experience listening to sounds with and without the earmuffs. When they come back into class, they could draw a picture and write about their experience.

Activity notes and answers

Page 122 Talk partners Listen to learners discussing why the animals have such big ears. Accept learners' answers, particularly since they might not know much about the animals in the pictures. They will therefore be using their own experience to suggest reasons.

Page 122 Activity 1
a Learners could use books and posters, or access pictures filed on the computer by you.
b Ask learners to draw the animals, paying attention to the ears.
c Some animals have *big* ears to help them to *hear* better.

Earmuffs

 Activity notes and answers

Page 123 Activity 1 Challenge learners to use the scientific words that they have been learning as they describe what happens, such as *sound*, *source of sound* and *ears*.

Page 123 Activity 2

a and **b** Prompt learners to compare what they can hear with and without the earmuffs. Ask them to think about how wearing the earmuffs changes sounds.

c Encourage learners to use comparative language, such as *louder*, *quieter*, *clearer* and *muffled*. If some learners are unsure of language to describe the sounds, provide and explain words on cards that they could use.

d When learners repeat this activity outdoors, firstly ask them to walk around and listen without the earmuffs on and then compare what they hear with the earmuffs on. Challenge learners to use comparative language, such as *louder* and *quieter*, as well as *fainter*.

e Accept appropriate sentences based on learners' experiences, such as: *When I put on the earmuffs, the sounds are muffled, quiet, faint, strange.*

Further activities

- Show learners the Unit 6 digital resource video clip 1: Fennec fox. Draw attention to the size of the fox's ears and how they move as it listens.

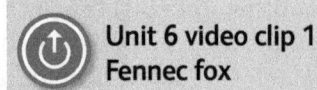
Unit 6 video clip 1: Fennec fox

- Ask learners to complete the Unit 6 digital resource PCM2: Ears.

 Unit 6 PCM2: Ears

Answers to PCM2:

1 The large ears mean they have very good hearing which helps them to hear prey. (They can even hear underneath the ground.)

2 For example, elephant, bat, hare.

3 To hear better, to hear from different directions.

- Ask learners to complete Workbook page 73: What can you hear?
- Give learners pictures of people using ear defenders in the workplace, such as in an airport, using machinery in a factory or using pneumatic drills. Ask them to discuss and explain why it is important that these people wear ear defenders. Encourage them to think about why they need to block the sounds out.

Success criteria

While completing the activities, assess and record learners who can:

- identify many sources of sound in the classroom and school grounds
- know that we hear when sound enters our ear and that earmuffs block the sound
- try to answer questions by collecting evidence through observing different animal ears
- explore and observe using earmuffs to find out how sounds change
- make comparisons between listening to sounds with and without earmuffs.

 Workbook answers

Page 73 What can you hear?

1 Check learners' drawings and labels.

2 For example, I predict that *the sounds will be fainter.*

3 For example, loud sounds are dangerous because they can damage your ears.

4 a True **b** False

  c False **d** True

Looking after your ears 1

 Learner's Book
pages 124–125

 Workbook
page 74

Objectives

- Identify many sources of sound. (1Ps1)
- Know that we hear when sound enters our ear. (1Ps2)

Background information

Page 124 of the Learner's Book builds on the use of ear defenders to protect ears and hearing. It further develops learners' understanding of why they need to look after their ears, as well as what it might feel like to lose some or all of their hearing. There is a very useful saying in relation to looking after ears, 'You shouldn't put anything smaller than your elbow in your ear'. This is quite true – it is dangerous to put things into the ear; even a cotton earbud can do damage. Explain this to learners and share some basic care information, such as:

- Keep your ears clear. Wash them when you wash your face.
- Do not poke inside the ear with anything.
- Make sure you do not listen to very loud sounds.
- Never make loud noises next to someone's ear.
- If your ears hurt, tell your parents or carers who will take you to see the doctor.

The activities on page 125 focus on hearing and hearing loss. Humans have different levels of hearing: some hear very well, while others are born with limited or no hearing (deafness), which is permanent. Temporary hearing loss can be caused by a build-up of wax or a hearing infection (which some learners will have experienced) or by an object getting stuck in the ear canal (cotton buds are often the cause). Some people experience damage to their hearing because of disease, an accident or being close to a loud noise.

The loss of hearing affects people in different ways. For some, it means that it is less easy to communicate with others. They can feel alone and they cannot rely on their hearing to keep them safe, such as when crossing a road or hearing a knock at the door. Hearing aids can help. Some people also use sign language to communicate with other deaf people.

Some learners may have a hearing impairment or know someone who has. If they are happy to do so, encourage them to share their experiences with other learners. This will help to develop understanding and empathy among classmates, and tolerance of people who appear different in some way.

Starter activity suggestions

- Ask learners if anyone has ever been to the doctor about their ears. Did the doctor look inside their ears? What was the equipment like? (Explain that doctors are trained to use instruments to carefully check ears without causing damage. Emphasise again that learners should never put things in their own ears.)
- Share ideas about what the words *deaf*, *deafness*, *hearing impairment* and *hearing aid* mean. Some learners might know about these from experience. Develop shared definitions, which could be placed on display, or in a class dictionary/glossary.

Activity notes and answers

Page 124 Talk partners This could be a whole class activity, if you think that there are not enough learners who have had an ear infection.

a Listen to learners discussing what the doctor is doing. The name for the instrument is an otoscope or auriscope, which sees inside the ear canal. (Remind them that doctors are trained to use such ear instruments safely.)

b and **c** Ask learners if they have ever had earache. Let them share what it was like and what they had to do to make it better, such as using eardrops, or drinking syrup or tablets to clear up the infection. Ask learners to share why they may have had difficulty hearing, such as wax or an infection blocking sound.

Looking after your ears 2

 Activity notes and answers

Page 125 Talk partners
a and **b** Listen to learners discussing what they think it would be like to be deaf and which sounds they would miss. Their responses will be personal to themselves, so accept all answers.
c Some learners will be able to write a sentence to accompany their pictures.

Page 125 Activity 1 Accept reasonable answers. Encourage learners to think about themselves crossing roads, and how the hood acts like an earmuff, blocking sound. It would be dangerous for the boy to cross the road with his hood up.

Page 125 Activity 2 If you used the video from the Starting Points section, you could show a sequence where the children are explaining signs and then practise signing using the signs on the page. Give learners the opportunity to sign to each other and check if they understand what they are signing.

Further activities

- Ask learners to complete Workbook page 74: Looking after your ears.

- If you know someone who is hearing impaired and uses sign language and lip reading, invite them to visit your class, so that they can share their experiences with the learners and answer their questions.

- Make a display of photographs of each learner in the class. Place a speech bubble next to each photo, in which learners can write (or you write) the sound that they would miss if they could not hear.

- Ask learners to make a poster to tell others how to look after their ears.

- In a school assembly, ask learners to teach other classes how to sign hello, goodbye, thank you, and so on.

 ICT links
Learners could video themselves signing for other class members to work out what they are signing.

Success criteria

While completing the activities, assess and record learners who can:
- say which sounds they would miss if they could not hear
- say that we hear when sound enters our ear.

 Workbook answers
Page 74 Looking after your ears
1 a, b and c Check learners' drawings.

Helping us to hear

 Learner's Book
pages 126–127

 Workbook
page 75

 Digital Resource

Objectives

- Identify many sources of sound. (1Ps1)
- Know that we hear when sound enters our ear. (1Ps2)
- Try to answer questions by collecting evidence through observation. (1Ep1)
- Decide what to do to try to answer a science question. (1Ep4)
- Suggest ideas and follow instructions. (1Eo2)
- Record stages in work. (1Eo3)

Background information

The activities on page 126 of the Learner's Book expand learners' understanding of sound, as well as consolidate learning about identifying sources of sound. The activities use the idea of listening to heartbeats to reinforce that we hear when sound enters our ears.

The activities on page 127 revisit the idea of sources of sound, so that it is reinforced and becomes embedded. It is also an opportunity for you to assess which learners have mastered this concept.

Starter activity suggestions

- If you have stethoscopes as part of the school's science resources, learners could explore using them and talk about what they can hear. Remind learners that they need to stay still and be quiet so that they can hear the sounds.

- Show learners the Unit 6 digital resource video clip 2: Using a stethoscope, which shows a doctor using a stethoscope on a child. Ask learners how they think the stethoscope works, by asking questions such as: *Why is the doctor using it? Will the sound be louder or quieter through the stethoscope?*

 Unit 6 video clip 2: Using a stethoscope

- Ask the class if anyone has had a doctor use a stethoscope on them, why they went to the doctor and what they think the doctor was listening to.

- Ask learners to talk with their partners about what part of the body the doctor is listening to and what sounds these body parts make, such as listening to the lungs and someone breathing, or to the heart and heartbeat.

 ## Activity notes and answers

Page 126 Activity 1

a Listen to learners discussing how the stethoscope was made. If possible, give them access to resources so that they can explore and see how the parts might fit together. Give support to any learners who may be having difficulty in working out how to make their own stethoscope. The learners taped the funnel to the end of the cardboard tube.

b and c Learners make the stethoscope and explore using it to listen to their partner's heartbeat. Make sure that learners know where on the body they need to place the stethoscope to hear the heart.

Page 126 Activity 2

a Learners describe what they hear using the stethoscope. Some learners might describe the rustle of clothing, because they could not find the heartbeat.

b For example: The heartbeat sounded like a drum. A stethoscope helps a doctor to hear the heart beating.

Page 126 Challenge yourself! Encourage learners to think about how they could change the stethoscope. For example, would a longer tube, or a larger cone at the end, be better?

A day in the life of my ears

 Activity notes and answers

Page 127 Activity 1 Learners might find it helpful if you complete a day in the diary as a class, so that the diary is modelled and learners understand what a diary is used for.

Further activities

- Ask learners to complete Workbook page 75: Using a stethoscope.

- Ask learners to carry out a survey across the school to find out how many learners in each class have had a doctor use a stethoscope on them. Each group could be allocated a class to visit, which has been arranged with the respective class teachers. Collect the data and with the class make a pictograph, perhaps using stethoscope pictures to represent each child.

- Give learners the opportunity to look at their partner's diary and compare it with their own. Ask them to look for similarities and differences between the two diaries.

Success criteria

While completing the activities, assess and record learners who can:

- identify many sources of sound
- say that we hear when sound enters our ear
- try to answer questions about how a stethoscope works by using it themselves
- decide what to do to try to answer the question about how the stethoscope was made
- suggest ideas and follow instructions (through looking at the picture) on how to make a stethoscope
- record a day in the life of their ears by using a diary.

 Workbook answers

Page 75 Using a stethoscope

1 *The doctor can hear my heartbeat or me breathing.*

2 Accept, for example, heartbeat, breathing, coughing, rustling.

3 Accept, for example, heart, lungs, clothes.

Moving away from sound

Learner's Book
pages 128–129

Workbook
page 76

Objectives

- Identify many sources of sound. (1Ps1)
- Know that we hear when sound enters our ear. (1Ps2)
- Recognise that as sound travels from a source it becomes fainter. (1Ps3)
- Explore and observe in order to collect evidence (measurements and observations) to answer questions. (1Eo1)
- Suggest ideas and follow instructions. (1Eo2)
- Make comparisons. (1Eo4)

Background information

The activities on pages 128 and 129 of the Learner's Book introduce the idea that the further away from an object you are, the fainter the sound becomes. This may sound like a simple concept; however, some learners think that the source of the sound itself makes the sound quieter, rather than the distance.

When you are standing close to the source of the sound, it seems loud. As you move away from the source of the sound, it seems quieter. In fact, the source is still producing the sound at the same volume. It is the distance that is affecting how loud the sound seems.

When learners carry out Activity 1 on page 128, you can help them to understand this by asking the person making a sound with the shaker to make sure that the sound stays at the same volume as the partner moves away.

Starter activity suggestions

- If possible, show learners a video clip from the internet that shows what happens when you move away from the source of a sound.
- Play a simple musical instrument (such as a triangle) at the front of the class. Now move away from the class out into the corridor, still playing your instrument, then go back into the classroom. Ask learners to describe what happened to the sound. If necessary, model comparative language, such as *fainter* and *louder*. Impress upon the class that you did not change the volume (loudness) of the instrument – you kept it the same when you were walking. This will help to develop their understanding that it is the distance from the source of sound that makes the sound seem quieter.

Activity notes and answers

Page 128 Activity 1

a As learners follow the set of instructions to make their own shaker. Encourage learners to help each other. Check that learners are able to follow the instructions correctly, but allow them to customise their shaker with patterns as they wish.

b Learners working in pairs should have decided that one person makes the sound and the other walks away, until they can no longer hear the sound. This activity is best carried out in the school grounds, where there is plenty of space and learners are not distracted by other groups.

c The reason for learners swapping is twofold: to make sure that everyone experiences each part of the activity, and so that the learners share experiences, comparing them to see if they were the same or different. This enables them to draw a conclusion.

d *When I moved away from the sound, it got fainter.*

Sounds near and far

 Activity notes and answers

Page 129 Activity 1
a Accept appropriate answers, such as people talking or walking along the corridor.
b Accept appropriate answers, such as cars, planes, or doors banging.
c Check that learners' answers are appropriate.

Page 129 Challenge yourself! Some learners might be challenged when having to work out the combinations of far away but loud. Prompt them by getting them to remember the shaker activity on page 128. The sound was loud to the person using the shaker, but not to the person who has moved away.

Further activities

- Ask learners to complete Workbook page 76: Sounds near and far.
- Give learners the opportunity to explore different sources of sound, other than their shakers, and repeat Activity 1 from Learner's Book page 128. Challenge learners to think about how they could measure the distance at which they stopped hearing the sound.
- Play a game with the class. One learner stands outside the classroom door. You or a classmate hides something that makes a sound (such as a ticking clock, but not too loud). When the learner comes back in, they have to listen carefully and find the sound by moving around in the class. Talk to learners about this being the opposite to the shaker activity – the sound seems louder the closer you get to it.
- Tell learners that when they go home, they could write lists or sentences or take photographs of things that make loud sounds and get fainter as they move away, such as a car.

 ICT links

The activity on Learner's Book page 128 provides an opportunity to assess how well learners can follow a set of instructions to make their shaker.

Success criteria

While completing the activities, assess and record learners who can:
- identify many sources of sound, such as a ticking clock
- know that we hear when sound enters our ear
- say that as sound travels from a source it becomes fainter, and that they know this because when they move away from a sound, it gets fainter
- carry out their idea to answer questions
- follow instructions to make their shaker
- make comparisons of how loud the sound is as they move away from the source of the sound.

 Workbook answers

Page 76 Sounds near and far
1 a tambourine, cymbals, whistle
  b feather shaker, tapping sticks
  c Chen could hit them harder.

Sounds getting fainter

 Learner's Book
pages 130–131

 Workbook
page 77

 Digital Resource

Objectives

- Identify many sources of sound. (1Ps1)
- Know that we hear when sound enters our ear. (1Ps2)
- Recognise that as sound travels from a source it becomes fainter. (1Ps3)
- Decide what to do to try to answer a science question. (1Ep4)
- Explore and observe in order to collect evidence (measurements and observations) to answer questions. (1Eo1)
- Make comparisons. (1Eo4)

Background information

The activities on pages 131 and 132 of the Learner's Book consolidate learners' understanding of the idea that as sound travels from a source, it becomes fainter. Learners also use and further develop their scientific enquiry skills.

On page 131, they carry out a simple comparative test, following a simple set of instructions and placing a marker down, so that they can compare the distance to draw a conclusion. On page 132, the comparative test is extended. Learners measure using non-standard measures (counting steps) to decide if they hear the sound at the same distance. Give learners the choice of how to measure. If some choose standard measures, allow this and provide support where needed.

Starter activity suggestions

- Take the class out into the school grounds. Explain to them that you are going to make a sound. You will keep the sound the same as they walk away. When they can no longer hear the sound, they should stop. Tell them not to worry if they stop before other classmates. Ask them to form a line, standing next to each other with their backs to you. Begin making the sound and tell them to start walking. When all learners have stopped, end the sound and walk to face the class, making sure that they stay in position. Ask learners to think about what happened to the sound as they walked away from it, and also why different learners stopped in different places.

- Display the Unit 6 digital resource slideshow, slide 6: Sounds getting fainter. Use it to elicit ideas from the class and assess whether or not they are able to suggest a simple comparative test, based on their experience so far.

 Unit 6 slideshow, slide 6: Sounds getting fainter

Answers to slide 6:

a For example, *Work with someone, they make a sound and the other person slowly walks away and stops when they cannot hear the sound.*

b This activity is better carried out outdoors with learners working in pairs. Suggest to the class that the learner who walks away from the sound takes a pencil and paper to write down how many steps they took.

c At this stage, most learners will be using non-standard measures so counting steps is appropriate. If you have a trundle wheel learners could use it and count the number of clicks.

 Activity notes and answers

Page 130 Activity 1 Check that learners are following the instructions carefully. If any learners have problems, read the instructions with them and ask them to repeat what they have to do.

Page 130 Talk partners
Example answers:
a *The sound got fainter the further away we walked from the source of the sound.*
b *We both stopped at the same/different place.*
c *We think the same thing would happen.*
d Accept appropriate answers, such as: *The sound was the same/different; we took the same steps as last time.*

How far?

 Activity notes and answers

Page 131 Activity 1
a and b Check that the learners are able to count the number required. If you think some learners are not
   confident in counting, put them into groups of three so that one of them can count the steps.
c Learners could use paper or a mini-whiteboard to record the number of steps.

Page 131 Talk partners Listen to learners' discussions. Use this as an assessment opportunity to find out if
they can apply their understanding that as sound travels from a source, it sounds fainter.

Page 131 Activity 2
a and b Accept answers that are reasonable and relate to the helicopter being the source of sound. It is
   much louder than a drum, so you would have to walk further away before you could not hear it.

Further activities

- Ask learners to complete Workbook page 77: Sounds getting fainter.
- Display the Unit 6 digital resource slideshow, slide 7: Sound results. Use it to see if learners recognise that
  the children carried out a similar test to the ones they have been doing. Ask them additional questions such
  as: *What did the other class do that was the same and different to what you did? How did the class measure
  the distance?*

 Unit 6 slideshow, slide 7: Sound results

Answers to slide 7:
a Accept reasonable responses, such as: *Worked with someone, they made a sound and the other person
   slowly walked away and stopped when they could not hear the sound.*
b Lin   c Sam 18 steps

- Divide the class into groups of four. Ask them to copy what the children on slide 7 did, and ask them how
  they would record the number of steps. Then take one group's data and use it to create a graph on the
  interactive whiteboard, and if possible, ask the class to help you create it.

Success criteria

While completing the activities, assess and record learners who can:
- identify the source of sound in their activities
- understand that we hear when sound enters our ear
- recognise that as sound travels from a source it becomes fainter
- decide what to do to find out what happens when you move away
  from a sound
- measure how many steps they took before they could not hear
  the sound
- make comparisons between how many steps each person took.

 Workbook answers

Page 77 Sounds getting
fainter
1 a Tom
  b 20 steps
  c Check learners'
    drawings.

Sounds from far away

 Learner's Book
pages 132–133

 Workbook
page 78

Objectives

- Identify many sources of sound. (1Ps1)
- Recognise that as sound travels from a source it becomes fainter. (1Ps3)
- Make predictions. (1Ep3)
- Decide what to do to try to answer a science question. (1Ep4)
- Explore and observe in order to collect evidence (measurements and observations) to answer questions. (1Eo1)
- Compare what happened with predictions. (1Eo5)
- Model and communicate ideas in order to share, explain and develop them. (1Eo6)

Background information

The activity on page 132 of the Learner's Book provides an opportunity for learners to apply their understanding of the idea that as sound travels from a source, it becomes fainter. This is done through learners using scientific enquiry skills when they sort a collection of sound makers into two groups, and predict whether they think they will be able to hear them far away or not. They then use their scientific enquiry skills to carry out a comparative test to find out if their predictions were correct. This could be further extended if learners were paired with another group to model what they did to explain what happened.

The activity on page 133 of the Learner's Book reverses the activity for learners when they make a sound maker and challenge another group to find out how far away it can be heard. The group then has to report back to the learners who made the sound maker, developing skills of communication and explanation.

Starter activity suggestions

- Provide a set of sound makers (sources of sound), a large enough collection so that learners can choose at least five different ones to use in their activity. Challenge learners to choose five sources of sound that they think they will hear far away and some closer.
- Give learners time to sort their collection, making sure that their groups have labels. Then pair up groups to go and look at the other pair's groups. They should leave a comment on a sticky note stating whether they agree or do not agree, and which ones they think are in the wrong set. Learners who do not have written language could use smiley and frown faces.

Activity notes and answers

Page 132 Activity 1

a and **b** The sets learners decide upon will depend on the sources of sound chosen. Accept their predictions, as they are going to test if they are correct.

c, d and **e** The outcomes will depend on their predictions. Discuss with learners what they found out, and if they can offer a reason why some sources of sound should go into a different set. Challenge learners to move incorrect suggestions into the correct set.

Make your own sound makers

Page 133 Activity 1 Check that learners have used materials that will make both quiet and loud sounds.

Page 133 Activity 2 Each pair in the class will carry out this activity and report back to another pair, so the learners will be carrying out this activity for someone else. Observe learners carrying out the activity and listen to them reporting back in relation to the learning outcomes and success criteria.

Further activities

- Ask learners to complete Workbook page 78: Sound words.
- Ask learners to bring things from home (with permission) to try out, such as whistles.
- Ask learners to think about and try to make a sound maker that can be heard by their partner further away than anything they have tried so far.

Success criteria

While completing the activities, assess and record learners who can:

- identify sources of sound
- recognise that as sound travels from a source, it becomes fainter
- predict which objects they will or will not be able to hear from far away
- decide what to do to find out how far away a sound can be heard
- measure distance to answer their question on how far away they could hear a sound
- compare what happened with their predictions
- demonstrate and explain to others what they did and explain what they found out.

 Workbook answers

Page 78 Sound words
1 a For example:
   quack – duck
   howl – wolf
   hiss – snake
   buzz – bee
   fizz – drink
   tick – clock
   pop – balloon
   clap – hands
   hoot – owl
   ring – bell
   crunch – potato chips
   click – fingers
 b For example: ping, bang, clank, beep, chirp, drip, growl.

Sound effects

 Learner's Book
pages 134–136

 Workbook
page 79

Objectives

- Identify many sources of sound. (1Ps1)
- Know that we hear when sound enters our ear. (1Ps2)

Background information

The activities on pages 134 and 135 of the Learner's Book link science with literacy as a way of learners applying their understanding of sound from this unit in a different and creative context.

Discuss what sound effects are with the class, explaining that they are used to make sounds on TV programmes and some radio programmes, to make what viewers see and listen to sound more realistic. To do this, the people who create sound effects cannot always use the real thing, such as a horse. They have to use something that sounds like it, such as the classic tapping of two coconut shells together for the sound of the horse's hooves.

In making poems, you could introduce learners to onomatopoeia – special words that imitate sounds, such as drip and splash.

The activities on page 135 challenge learners to apply the idea of sound effects to accompany a story. As learners work, use this as an assessment opportunity by asking them what the source of the sound is, how they will make it, is the sound close or far away, and which sense the audience will use to hear the sound.

The activities on page 136 offer an opportunity to revisit a selection of the ideas developed in this unit.

Starter activity suggestions

- Use video clips which show a picture and the accompanying sound. Ask learners how they would make sound effects, such as water noises or animal sounds.
- Give groups a collection of materials that they could use to make sound effects, such as plastic bottles, stones, wooden blocks, and glass paper (sand paper). Put actions on the board, such as someone hammering and a door creaking. Challenge learners to use the materials to make the sound effects. They can then share them with the rest of the class, who could comment on how realistic the sound effects were.

 ### Activity notes and answers

Page 134 Activity 1 Accept learners' responses, such as crunching paper up to make the sound of someone eating an apple, or stamping on the floor to suggest someone walking.

Page 134 Activity 2 This could be developed as a class poem where sound words are given to the class and learners contribute through discussion. It could be based on children themselves, such as talking, walking, whispering, playing.

A sound story

 ### Activity notes and answers

Page 135 Activity 1 Listen to learners as they work. Provide support where appropriate. They could make up their own story or use a traditional tale. Some learners can get carried away, so you might need to give a time limit to their story and also steer learners away from overly violent tales.

Page 135 Activity 2 Give learners time to tell their story to the rest of the class. Sometimes sharing all stories in one session can be too much for young learners, so you could spread out the stories over several days. After each story, ask other members of the class to comment on which sound effects they thought were very good.

Page 135 Activity 3 Learners could either video or audio record their story to play for other classes. Ask teachers in the other classes to encourage the audience to give feedback.

What have you learnt about sound?

Page 136 Activity 1 Check that learners have sorted the sounds that they have heard appropriately.

Page 136 Activity 2

Answers:

radio	kettle whistling	parent and child talking	cat meowing

Further activities

- Ask learners to complete Workbook page 79: Sound poem.
- Learners could give a sound performance during a school gathering or to another class.
- Encourage learners to go home and make up their own play with sound effects to bring back to class to show the others.

Success criteria

While completing the activities, assess and record learners who can:

- identify different sources of sound and use them to make sound effects
- know that we hear when sound enters our ear.

Assessment ideas

Ask learners to self-assess using the 'What can you remember?' checklist on page 136 of the Learner's Book, as well as the self-assessment table on page 80 of the Workbook.

Ask learners to complete Quiz 3 on pages 137–138 in the Learner's Book.

 Workbook answers

Page 79 Sound poem

1 Quack Quack goes the d*uck*
Chirp Chirp goes the *chick*
Brmm Brmm goes the c*ar*
Ring Ring goes the *bell*
Tick tock goes the *clock*
What a lot of noise!

2 Accept reasonable responses.

Quiz 3 Physics

Answers:

1 **a** crawl   **b** swim   **c** fly   **d** bounce

2 **a** push   **b** pull   **c** push

3 **a** speeding up   **b** slowing down   **c** changing direction.

4 Accept reasonable responses.

5 Ears

6 *If you move away from the sound, it gets fainter.*

7 Accept, for example: *They have big ears so that they can hear better and catch food/prey/animals.*

8 **a–c** Accept all reasonable responses.

Name: ....

Tasting plant parts

1 Complete this table. An example has been done for you.

Plant	Part of plant	Soft	Crunchy	Hard	Juicy	Sweet	Like? ☺ ☹
celery	stem	✗	✓	✓	✗	✗	☺

Hodder Cambridge Primary Science Teacher's Pack 1 ©Hodder & Stoughton Ltd 2017

Name: ....

All about Me

This is a page about you.

1 Complete the sentences.

   a My name is _____. I am _____ years old.

   b The colour of my eyes is _____.

   c The colour of my hair is _____.

   d My favourite food is _____.

   e My favourite animal is _____.

   f When I grow up I want to be _____.

2 Here is a picture of my family.

Name: ....

Food swap

These children are thinking about what they would like to eat or drink.
Help them to think of healthy foods and drinks by drawing them instead.

Name: ....

Soft materials

tick soft materials onto Rabbit.

w many different soft materials can you use?

Name: ....

Pushes and pulls

1 a Go around the classroom. Make things move by pushing or pulling them. Each time you use a push, say *push*. Each time you make something move with a pull, say *pull*.

  b Draw pictures of what you did in these circles.

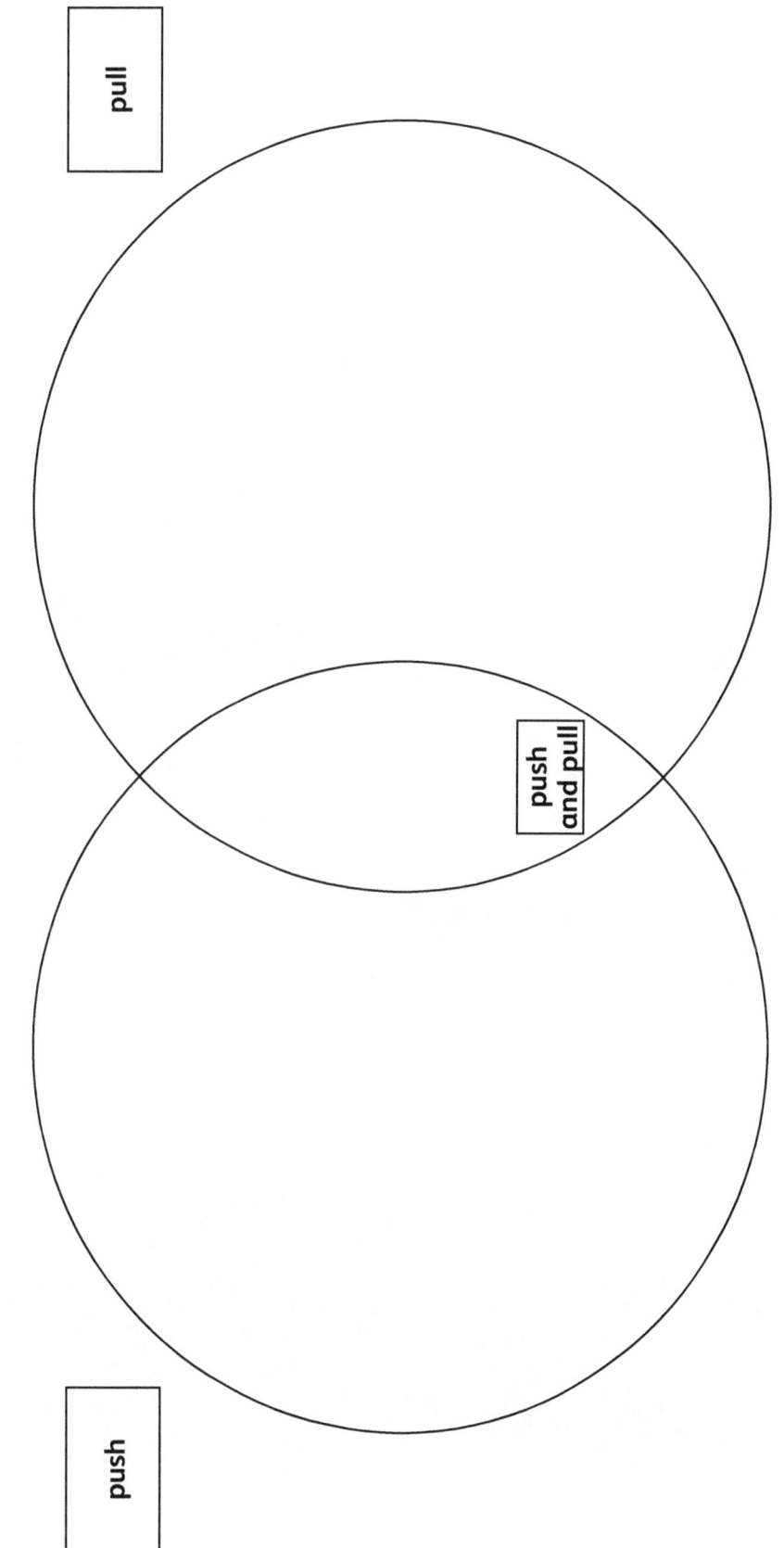

push

push and pull

pull

Hodder Cambridge Primary Science Teacher's Pack 1 ©Hodder & Stoughton Ltd 2017

Sources of sound

1 Look at this picture. Put a circle around everything that is a source of sound.